Collins

Happy handwriting

Teacher's Guide 6

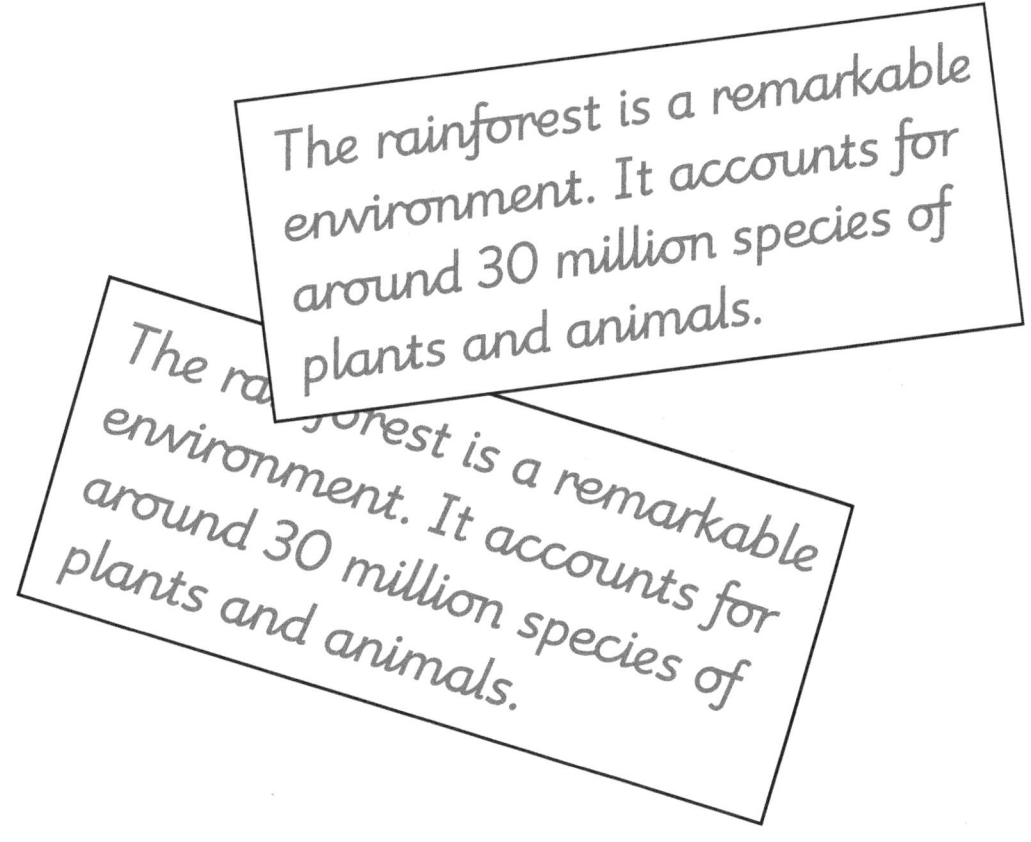

Series Editor: Dr Jane Medwell
Author: Stephanie Austwick

William Collins' dream of knowledge for all began with the publication of his first book in 1819.
A self-educated mill worker, he not only enriched millions of lives, but also founded a flourishing publishing house. Today, staying true to this spirit, Collins books are packed with inspiration, innovation and practical expertise.
They place you at the centre of a world of possibility and give you exactly what you need to explore it.

Collins. Freedom to teach.

Published by Collins
An imprint of HarperCollins*Publishers*
The News Building, 1 London Bridge Street, London, SE1 9GF, UK

HarperCollins*Publishers*
1st Floor, Watermarque Building, Ringsend Road, Dublin 4, Ireland

Browse the complete Collins catalogue at
collins.co.uk

© HarperCollins*Publishers* Limited 2022

10 9 8 7 6 5 4 3 2 1

ISBN 978-0-00-848578-8

All rights reserved. No part of this publication may be reproduced, stored in a retrieval system, or transmitted in any form by any means, electronic, mechanical, photocopying, recording or otherwise, without the prior written permission of the Publisher or a licence permitting restricted copying in the United Kingdom issued by the Copyright Licensing Agency Ltd, 5th Floor, Shackleton House, 4 Battle Bridge Lane, London SE1 2HX.

British Library Cataloguing-in-Publication Data
A catalogue record for this publication is available from the British Library.

Series editor: Dr Jane Medwell
Author (lesson plans): Stephanie Austwick
Expert reviewer: Dr Mellissa Prunty
Publisher: Lizzie Catford
Product manager: Sarah Thomas
Project manager: Jayne Jarvis
Development editor: Jane Cotter
Copyeditor: Jilly Hunt
Proofreader: Claire Throp
Additional Practice sheet design template and icons: Sarah-Leigh Wills at Happydesigner

Cover designer: Sarah-Leigh Wills at Happydesigner
Illustrations: Jouve India Pvt. Ltd.
Typesetter: Jouve India Pvt. Ltd.
Production controller: Alhady Ali

Printed and bound in the UK using 100% renewable electricity at CPI Group (UK) Ltd.

MIX
Paper from responsible sources
FSC™ C007454

This book is produced from independently certified FSC™ paper to ensure responsible forest management. For more information visit:
www.harpercollins.co.uk/green

Contents

Handwriting: an important aspect of the modern curriculum	4
The *Happy Handwriting* course	6
Writing a school handwriting policy	8
Handwriting in the National Curriculum for Upper Key Stage 2	10
The teaching focus for each week (Year 6)	11
Letter formations	12
Teaching handwriting in Year 6	13
Teaching the *Happy Handwriting* lessons	15
Lesson plans: Units 1–10	17
Lesson plans: Units 11–20	27
Lesson plans: Units 21–30	37
Additional practice sheets	47
Assessing handwriting in Year 6	62
Handwriting example record sheet	67
Assessment record sheet for Year 6 handwriting	68
Assessment record sheet for joins in Year 6	69
Diagnostic assessment of handwriting sheet	70
Speed and fluency practice sheets	71
Extra practice sheet: diagonal joins	74
Extra practice sheet: horizontal joins	75
Extra practice sheet: joins to round letters	76
Extra practice sheet: capital letters for proper nouns	77
Guidance for alphabetical order tasks	78
Four-line writing guidelines: larger	79
Four-line writing guidelines: smaller	80

Handwriting: an important aspect of the modern curriculum

Handwriting that is efficient, fluent and readable is the basis of successful writing – it allows children to compose what they want to say. Handwriting is not only a medium through which much of the curriculum is learned, but it also helps children to learn a range of important aspects of the curriculum:

- In the early years, the link between handwriting of letters and phonics embeds phonological knowledge.
- Efficient and automatic letter production contributes to the quality of what is written. Handwriting has been called 'language by hand'.
- As children get older, handwriting helps them learn the patterns of morphemes and letters, which are the basis of effective spelling.
- Learning to use a 'range of hands' lets writers allocate attention to activities like note-making, drafting and high-quality presentation.
- Looking critically at their own handwriting enables children to identify strengths and weaknesses, and improve their presentation.
- When handwriting is well established, older writers may develop their own style, as part of their academic identity.

Efficient handwriting is the foundation of learning in school and all children are entitled to be taught how to write effectively and legibly. *Happy Handwriting* offers children a carefully designed route to efficient, effective handwriting, using the simplest possible pathway.

Happy Handwriting

The content and structure of *Happy Handwriting* is based on a wide range of research into handwriting conducted around the world. This emphasises that direct teaching of a carefully structured handwriting programme is the best way to ensure children learn automatic handwriting as efficiently as possible.

Evidence from handwriting research emphasises the importance of consistency and continuity in handwriting teaching. *Happy Handwriting* is a carefully developed progression from correct letter movements and joins in KS1, to consolidation of joins, size and spacing in Years 3 and 4. In Upper Key Stage 2, *Happy Handwriting* promotes the consolidation of difficult joins, placing and spacing of letters and punctuation marks, aspects of proofreading and the development of personal style. Throughout Key Stage 2, *Happy Handwriting* develops children's abilities to write at different speeds depending on the writing task, so that they can learn to make decisions about when to prioritise neatness or speed, but always aim for legibility. These skills need regular, direct teaching and practice, which is presented in the children's books, presentations, teachers' guidance and planning for each week. These resources build consistency and clarity in lessons and also mean children acquire effective learning routines.

Not all children will learn with the same level of ease or at the same rate. It is important for both children and teachers to make assessments of the key aspects of handwriting progress and offer targeted practice to consolidate skills. In Years 5 and 6, children who struggle with automatic letter production or joining may find that their handwriting hinders their access to the curriculum or inhibits composition. *Happy Handwriting* provides appropriate assessment points, diagnostic materials and recording sheets for teachers to identify children who need more support and offers additional practice materials.

Happy Handwriting provides teaching and practice materials, but also asks you to assess handwriting outside handwriting lessons, as this is the ultimate criterion for successful learning of handwriting.

Key principles of Happy Handwriting

- *Happy Handwriting* sees handwriting as 'language by hand' and recognises that efficient, automatic letter generation contributes to the quality of what children write.
- *Happy Handwriting* teaches a simple, modern cursive font with exit strokes (or flicks) from the very start, to prepare the children for efficient joined handwriting. You can use this font to prepare materials or displays for children or to make additional worksheets.
- *Happy Handwriting* is a planned, cumulative programme of skills teaching which involves regular review and assessment, so that teaching can be adjusted to meet the child's needs.
- *Happy Handwriting* teaches the correct letter movement for each letter right from the start. This is the most effective way to develop a 'hand habit' that prepares for joined handwriting.
- If children learn the correct letter movement as a 'hand habit' it will become automatic, so that they do not need to allocate cognitive attention to it. In reading, we aim for all children to learn sound–symbol correspondences to the point where they are automatic and in writing, we want children to produce letter movements automatically. This takes practice, so *Happy Handwriting* provides the materials to practise handwriting 'little and often' and encourages parents and carers to do small amounts of practice at home.
- *Happy Handwriting* teaches the efficient joins between letters as early as possible.
- Adult handwriting joins letters for efficient writing, but adult handwriting does not join every letter. *Happy Handwriting* teaches joined handwriting using the efficient joins but does not join 'break' letters, as that reduces writing efficiency.
- In Years 5 and 6, *Happy Handwriting* teaches children to write quickly and legibly, so that they can choose when to prioritise speed in their writing.
- In Years 5 and 6, *Happy Handwriting* offers diagnostic assessment materials to facilitate identification of children who will benefit from using the additional resources in the Teacher's Guide and printable resources. In this way, the needs of individuals and groups can be addressed.
- *Happy Handwriting* teaches letter names and alphabetical order so that you can talk about lower-case and capital letters, as well as spelling, and introduce children to resources like dictionaries.
- *Happy Handwriting* introduces proofreading to older writers, to build good writing habits.
- *Happy Handwriting* promotes the efficient use of resources to maximise teaching time and support teachers' preparation and assessment.

The *Happy Handwriting* course

Happy Handwriting provides guidance and resources for you to teach efficient, fluent and legible handwriting as simply as possible, and to create a clear, shared handwriting policy in school. *Happy Handwriting* teaches the key elements of early handwriting: letter movements, alphabet knowledge, joins between letters and well-proportioned writing as early and thoroughly as possible. The course then supports writing at different speeds and with different attention to neatness depending on the circumstances. Finally, *Happy Handwriting* promotes the development of an efficient personal style of writing.

Handwriting should be taught specifically, and separately from phonics or spelling instruction. However, letter formation and knowledge of letter names contributes to phonics and literacy learning. Children who can form letters correctly and automatically, and can discuss the letters by their names, can use these skills in their spelling and writing. The teaching of correct letter movements early in children's literacy learning is an important foundation of fluent and automatic handwriting. By Years 5 and 6, all children should know the letter names and alphabetical order but if any children do struggle with these aspects of handwriting it is not too later to intervene and improve their performance, which will help with simple tasks like dictionary use, as well as handwriting.

In Year 5 and Year 6, most children will have learned the correct movements for letters and the main joins used in *Happy Handwriting*. They will need to practise controlling the size and relative proportions of letters and learn to make the trickier joins between letters automatically and smoothly. They will also learn to make choices about when to 'speed up' their writing, with the inevitable trade off with neatness, but retain legibility. In Year 5 and Year 6, *Happy Handwriting* also addresses printing in lower case and block capitals.

Some children will find learning handwriting relatively easy, and a few may almost seem to 'catch' it effortlessly. However, other children will find handwriting challenging and need more practice and attention. *Happy Handwriting* builds in regular self-review of handwriting by children and assessment by teachers, and you can use the additional resources to identify and support children who need more guided practice. There is assessment advice and recording sheets for handwriting assessments, and printable materials for home activity to support children's handwriting development. Short bursts of practice at home can be very effective practice, especially when supervised by an adult or sibling.

Letter formation is a movement, not just a shape

There is a letter formation movement in *Happy Handwriting* for each letter. It is very important that children use this movement every time they write the letter, always starting in the right place. Learning the letter movements automatically is the basis of fluent handwriting, which does not demand cognitive attention from writers. On the sheet of letter formations, the dot is the starting point and each arrow represents a directional stroke. These are set out on page 12 of this guide so that you can identify any children who are inconsistent in their letter formation.

For children who know all the letter movements automatically, the relative height of letters is the next priority. In Key Stage 2, children should use an exercise book or the writing guidelines provided in this Teacher's Guide on pages 79 and 80, in addition to the Practice Book.

The *Happy Handwriting* course prioritises the introduction of the correct movements to form lower-case letters (letter formation), followed by their capital formations. The letters are introduced in order of letter movement families, based on the formation of the letters. If you have a child struggling with consistently writing one family of letters, there is additional practice material provided.

The letter formation families

The four families are:
- The Curly Caterpillar family: anti-clockwise round, exemplified by the letter c
  - c a d g o q
  - e s f
- The Long Ladder family: down and off in another direction, exemplified by the letter l
  - i l t
  - u y j k
- The Robot family: down and retrace upwards, exemplified by the letter r
  - r n m
  - h b p
- The Zigzag family: straight, sharp turn, exemplified by the letter z
  - v w x z

Letter formation for left-handers

The formation of some letters is slightly different for some left-handed children, who 'pull' the lines right to left, where right handers will 'push' lines left to right: the lower-case letters t and f and capital letters A, E, F, H, J and T.

Joining letters in Key Stage 2

In Key Stage 1, *Happy Handwriting* teaches five main joins between letters:

1. Diagonal joins to letters without ascenders (for example: *ai*)
2. Diagonal joins to letters with ascenders (for example: *ch*)
3. Horizontal joins to letters without ascenders (for example: *wa*)
4. Horizontal joins to letters with ascenders (for example: *wh*)
5. Joins to round (anti-clockwise) letters (for example: *ad*)

Most children learn to produce joins efficiently in upper KS1 and lower KS2, but some children in Year 6 may still be establishing these joins as automatic movements. *Happy Handwriting* in Years 5 and 6 offers additional practice of the tricky or less frequent joins. All Key Stage 2 writers also need to know which letters not to join for maximum efficiency, and to focus on the size and spacing of letters and joins.

Break letters

Happy Handwriting uses a lower-case script where most letters have an exit stroke or 'flick', then moves into a mostly joined script where joins are natural and promote fluency and flow in writing. In *Happy Handwriting*, these letters do not join to letters following them: b, g, j, p, q, x, y, z, s. Most adults use an efficient semi-joined script when they write, and *Happy Handwriting* prepares children to learn this as early as possible.

Learning the alphabet

Knowing the names of the letters helps with phonics and spelling. Call a letter by its name, rather than the sound associated with it. If children learn the letter name when they learn the movement for the lower-case letter, they can then learn the capital letter which has the same name. Alphabetical order of letter names is an easily learned sequence that lasts a lifetime. It enables children to use dictionaries and alphabetical order – and it is one system that is not changing in this digital age! *Happy Handwriting* encourages you to sing the classic alphabet song – even in Key Stage 2 – to ensure everyone is secure in their alphabet knowledge, and to do the additional alphabet activities on page 77 of this guide. There are even more alphabet activities available in the *Happy Handwriting* printable resources.

Writing a school handwriting policy

A handwriting policy for your school needs to include handwriting in all its forms – using pens, pencils and digital tools – and for all its purposes, from note-taking to special presentation. Today, we recognise that children need to develop legibility, fluency and speed in their handwriting and that neatness is not the only criterion for good handwriting. There is a trade-off between efficiency and neatness, and children will need to learn to consciously adjust the balance between these two important aspects of handwriting. The simple, efficient font used by *Happy Handwriting* makes this easier for children to achieve.

The process of developing a handwriting policy gives teachers the chance to discuss the criteria for a successful handwriting curriculum. To develop a handwriting policy, you will need to include all classroom staff in the discussion of: the goals of the school handwriting curriculum, the way the curriculum is to be taught, and how the impact of the teaching is to be assessed. These criteria are summarised as the intent, implementation and impact of the handwriting curriculum (Ofsted, 2019). To ensure you have addressed these issues in your policy, you can discuss the answers to these questions:

- Is your handwriting curriculum based on evidence-based practice?
- Is the handwriting curriculum both ambitious and designed to give all learners the skills needed to communicate by hand?
- Is the curriculum coherently planned and sequenced for cumulative acquisition of knowledge and skills?
- Do teachers have training and support to enable them to teach handwriting effectively?
- Do teachers have a good knowledge of the development of handwriting skills?
- Do teachers create an environment that optimises learning conditions?
- Do the resources and materials support a coherently planned curriculum?
- Do teachers present the subject matter clearly?
- Do teachers check children's understanding systematically, identify misconceptions accurately and provide clear, direct feedback?
- Do teachers and leaders use assessment well, for example, to check understanding and inform teaching?

Happy Handwriting can be used to meet all these criteria, because it is systematically and cumulatively planned on the basis of research and evidence, and provides a full range of resources. *Happy Handwriting* sets ambitious goals for children's learning and provides additional materials for children who need them.

To develop a school policy, we recommend you should meet to discuss these aspects of the *Happy Handwriting* Teacher's Guide:

- the Collins Handwriting font – its features and where you can use it in school materials
- the order of introduction of letter movements and joins
- lesson processes and use of the *Happy Handwriting* resources in class
- assessment and recording
- using the *Happy Handwriting* additional materials to promote progress
- additional practice and parent/carer involvement activities.

An example of a school handwriting policy is included in the printable materials for discussion.

A handwriting policy should include, but not be limited to, the following content, which is discussed in this Teacher's Guide:

- the handwriting scheme used in school (including letter formations and joins)
- handwriting in the curriculum (what standards of presentation you have agreed)
- language about handwriting to promote clarity
- key issues in teaching handwriting
- resources used in school
- school approaches to teaching handwriting
- organisation of handwriting
- support for left-handed writers
- assessment of handwriting
- support for struggling writers
- involving parents and carers with handwriting.

The printable materials which are part of *Happy Handwriting* include:

- a chart of statutory assessment goals for handwriting and the goals of *Happy Handwriting*
- an example of a handwriting policy to discuss
- a glossary of terms about handwriting for each Key Stage so that both staff and children use a shared vocabulary and establish complete clarity about handwriting
- additional assessment and support materials.

You may want to develop a handwriting and presentation policy, commenting on presentation across the curriculum, or you may feel it is more useful to include presentation (and handwriting) in subject policies.

Glossary of terms (Key Stage 2)

- **Ascender**: the part of the letter that goes above the main body (t is shorter than others)
- **Baseline**: the line that the body of a short letter sits on
- **Bottom line**: the line in writing guidelines that descenders go down to
- **Break letter**: a letter that does not join to letters following it: b, g, j, p, q, x, y, z, s
- **Capital letter**: the term used in *Happy Handwriting* for upper-case letters
- **Cross bar**: the stroke going across t, f and some capitals
- **Descender**: the part of the letter that goes below the baseline
- **Diagonal join**: a join from the bottom of a letter
- **Exit stroke or flick**: letters that finish on the baseline may have a final flick in the forwards direction, which can become a join
- **Horizontal join**: a join from the top of a letter
- **Join**: the writing movement between one letter and the next; *Happy Handwriting* uses five main joins
- **Lower-case letter**: the term used in *Happy Handwriting* for a small letter
- **Memory phrase**: a mnemonic form of words to help remember lower-case letter formation
- **Round letter**: the round part of the letter body, where there is an anti-clockwise curve
- **Short letter** (or x-height letter): a letter without ascender or descender that is the same height as an *x*
- **Starting dot**: the point at which the letter should be started in order to facilitate good movement
- **Tall letter**: a letter with an ascender that goes to the top line of the guidelines.

Handwriting in the National Curriculum for Upper Key Stage 2

The National Curriculum for English programmes of study for writing at Key Stage 2 includes:

- transcription (spelling and handwriting)
- composition (articulating ideas and structuring them in speech and writing).

The Programmes of Study specify that, by the end of Year 6, children's reading and writing should be sufficiently fluent and effortless for them to manage the general demands of the curriculum in Year 7 and this includes automatic, effortless handwriting.

Statutory requirements (Upper Key Stage 2)

Pupils should be taught to 'write legibly, fluently and with increasing speed by choosing which shape of a letter to use when given choices and deciding whether or not to join specific letters; choosing the writing implement that is best suited for a task'.

Notes and guidance (non-statutory)

In Upper Key Stage 2, 'pupils should continue to practise handwriting and be encouraged to increase the speed of it, so that problems with forming letters do not get in the way of their writing down what they want to say. They should be clear about what standard of handwriting is appropriate for a particular task, for example, quick notes or a final handwritten version. They should also be taught to use an unjoined style where appropriate, for example, for labelling a diagram or data, writing an email address, or for algebra and capital letters, for example, for filling in a form.'

Teaching priorities for Happy Handwriting in Year 6

If children can learn fluent handwriting it will help them to write across the curriculum. The Year 6 priorities are:

- joining correctly where appropriate (and knowing where not to)
- consolidating difficult joins
- using appropriate spacing between letters and punctuation marks
- increasing speed
- choosing when to focus on speed, whilst retaining legibility
- placing and spacing punctuation correctly
- printing and using block capital letters when appropriate
- self-evaluating the formation, orientation, legibility and speed of their writing, according to task
- using first and second letter alphabetical order.

In Year 6 all children should be able to:

- produce letter movements automatically
- make joins automatically
- write ascenders and descenders consistently
- produce common letter combinations automatically.

The Year 6 Teacher's Guide contains advice and activities to diagnose the needs of children who may need more letter formation work to increase speed and automaticity. Additional activities for letter formation practice are available in the printable resources, and timed letter-generation games to practise automaticity are in the Teacher's Guide, pages 71–73.

The teaching focus for each week (Year 6)

Term 1	Handwriting focus
1	Writing quickly and writing neatly
2	Developing my own handwriting style and writing *f*
3	Joining to and from *r*
4	Slanting key joins: diagonal joins
5	Keeping ascenders and descenders parallel
6	Placing and spacing punctuation: sentence types
7	Writing quickly: words per minute
8	Writing neatly: a formal message
9	Writing brief notes about an event
10	Self-assessment
Term 2	
11	Spacing key joins: horizontal joins
12	Joining and breaking for descenders
13	Writing words with *qu*
14	Placing and spacing punctuation: apostrophes in contractions
15	Getting the height right: capital letters
16	Placing and spacing punctuation: commas and semi-colons
17	Writing quickly: making notes
18	Writing neatly and printing
19	Alphabetical order: advanced
20	Self-assessment
Term 3	
21	Spacing key joins: practising spacing and using compound words
22	Slanting your writing
23	Revising key joins: joins to round letters
24	Spacing tricky joins
25	Proofreading and paragraphing
26	Placing and spacing punctuation: commas, brackets and dashes
27	Writing quickly: instructions
28	Writing neatly
29	Proofreading, editing and improving
30	Self-assessment

Name/Group: _____ Date: _____

Letter formations

a b c d e f g

h i j k l m n

o p q r s t u

v w x y z

A B C D E F

G H I J K L M

N O P Q R S T

U V W X Y Z

Teaching handwriting in Year 6

Writing position

Good writing position allows writers to use their core and shoulder muscles for support and to move their arms. The writer's chair should be at a comfortable height so that they can place both feet flat on the floor for stability.

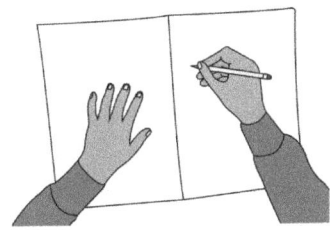

Right-handed children should place the paper or book slightly to the right and slant the paper slightly to the left. Right-handed children should steady the paper or book with their left hand.

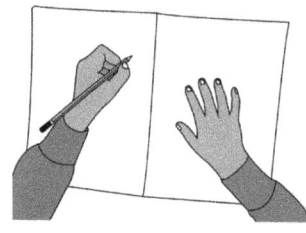

Left-handed children should place the paper or book slightly to the left and slant the paper slightly to the right. Left-handed children should steady the paper or book with their right hand.

Pencil (or pen) grip

To develop a fluent and fast handwriting style, children must develop a controlled pencil/pen grip that is comfortable for them. There are a number of perfectly acceptable ways to hold a pencil or pen, but many children hold the writing implement between the thumb and index finger with pencil/pen supported on the middle finger. The ring and little fingers are gently curled inwards. This gives an open, wide space, which means the movement comes from the fingers and produces a flexible hold which does not exhaust the writer. Any grip with a number of points of contact, and also some flexibility, is suitable if it is comfortable. Too tight a grip prevents free-flowing handwriting and is exhausting for the child. If children grip the pencil too tightly, they become tense in the arm and shoulder and place too much pressure on the paper, so this is something to watch for.

Hand preference

Around 10% of any population will prefer to write with their left hand. There are simple ways to support the details of posture, paper positioning, pencil grip, etc. that can make handwriting comfortable for all children, left- or right-handed.

Left-handed children

- Remember to model letter formation and joining specifically for left-handed children, with your left hand. You may also need to remind children which hand they write with.
- Left-handed children may benefit from sitting to the left of right-handed children to avoid elbow clashes.
- Left-handers may write better if they sit on a slightly higher chair so that they are further 'above' the writing.
- Left-handed children should tilt the paper to the right and steady the paper with a right hand. This takes practice.

- Left-handed children may benefit from holding the pencil/pen about 1.5 cm higher up the shaft than right-handed children. This helps prevents smudging, but is harder to control.
- Left-handed children may find that fountain pens dig into the paper, but can still enjoy using them.

Writing from left to right is more difficult for left-handed children because of the nature of our writing system. They may need more attention in the classroom to ensure that they do not learn bad habits of position, posture and pen hold, which will prevent development of fast, fluent and legible writing.

Choice of medium

Pencils are an ideal medium to start handwriting but, in Key Stage 2, a fibre-tipped pen that provides a good degree of friction gives young writers more control over their writing. Some types of 'slippery' ink in ballpoint pens can make good letter formation and joining even more difficult, so avoid these types of ink. In Year 6, writers may want to experiment with fountain pens and shaped nibs. These are not necessarily the most efficient implements, and might be best used on certain tasks, but they can add personal style and some fun to handwriting!

Teaching the Happy Handwriting lessons

Handwriting teaching routines

We recommend teaching at least two focused handwriting lessons per week for all children in Year 6, using the presentation and Practice Book. Each Unit has a handwriting and spelling focus built in. There are a range of additional activities that children in Year 6 can do.

For children who will benefit from more practice, the two main handwriting lessons can be supplemented with additional short practice sessions, to establish a join or letter movement. At Year 6, the *Happy Handwriting* course provides the following resources for each teaching week.

Happy Handwriting resource	Lesson goal	Location	Suggested for
Presentations	Introduction of joins and movements	Available to download	All lessons with the Practice Book
Practice Book (Lesson 1)	Introducing and practising the new material using the Practice Book	Practice Book and exercise book	All children
Practice Book (Lesson 2)	Practising the unit focus using the Practice Book	Practice Book and exercise book	All children
Home Practice sheets	Practising spellings and handwriting	Copiable resources in the Teacher's Guide	All children
Further practice	Practising the unit focus	Suggested activity in the weekly plan	Groups of children who may need to practise
Additional Practice sheets	Practising the unit focus using the sheet	Copiable sheets in the Teacher's Guide	Children struggling with this point
Extra Practice sheets	Practising the basic letter forms or joins to build fluency	Copiable sheets in the Teacher's Guide	Children struggling with fluency and automaticity, following diagnostic assessment
Printable Practice sheets	Revising and revisiting important basics	Copiable sheets in the Printable Resources for the year	Children struggling with fluency and automaticity, following diagnostic assessment

Start each lesson with a 'settling routine', including a short stretching routine to get the children's muscles ready to write. If any children do not know the alphabet, you may also want to sing the alphabet song, as it is an easy way to learn. Ensure the children are seated in the correct writing position at a table with their feet on the floor and their book or paper arranged so that they can write, and are gripping their pencils/pens appropriately.

The 'settling routine':

- stretch the arms above the head
- stretch arms out in front and wiggle fingers
- hunch and drop shoulders and push spine backwards
- rotate wrists and rotate ankles

- wriggle and stretch fingers
- ready to write!

During handwriting teaching, it is vital to observe the children in the act of writing so that you can check they are making the correct letter and join movements. These should be continuous, and children should not take the pencil/pen off the paper between letters. Dotting i or j or crossing t should be done when the word or letter sequence is finished.

Involving parents and carers in handwriting improvement

Handwriting benefits from regular, frequent practice, and most parents and carers are happy to support their children to do a short handwriting activity. A small, regular additional practice session can make a great deal of difference and does not provide too much challenge for most children. *Happy Handwriting* includes printable sheets suitable for children to complete at home, where any degree of encouragement from carers or other family members is helpful. Each sheet has a handwriting and spelling learning point, because spelling and handwriting practice can be usefully combined. The emphasis should be short bursts of practice, with plenty of praise, rather than completing the whole sheet.

Look Cover Write Check (LCWC)

Home handwriting sheets also have a spelling element because learning spelling and handwriting are complementary activities. When asking children in Year 6 to learn the spelling of words, we recommend using the Look Cover Write Check strategy.

LCWC involves:

- looking very carefully at the words and saying the name of each letter aloud (then shutting your eyes and 'seeing' the letters on your eyelids)
- covering up the word
- writing the word without looking back at it
- checking to see if it is correct.

The child can do this as many times as necessary. A folded 'fan' of paper (or book page) can give multiple opportunities.

Unit 1: Writing quickly and writing neatly

	Lesson 1	Lesson 2	Practice
	Class or groups seated at tables	*Class or groups seated at tables*	*Class or groups seated at tables*
Objectives	To discuss writing quickly versus writing neatly. To evaluate own speed writing.	To practise writing quickly and writing neatly. To evaluate own neat writing.	To consolidate writing quickly and writing neatly.
Resources	– Practice Book Page 3 – Presentation Part 1 – Pencil or pen	– Practice Book Page 3 – Presentation Part 2 – Pencil or pen	– Additional Practice sheet 1 – Presentation Part 3 – Pencil or pen – Timer – Handwriting book or lined paper

Teaching	• Settling routine and hand warm up
	• Use presentation to display and demonstrate the first set of words in the Practice Book.
	• **Practice Book:** Copy the words as quickly as possible.
	• Use presentation to discuss the quote from Hal, aged 11.
	• **Paired Talk:** Ask the children to discuss Hal's comments. *When might they need to use different types of handwriting? What are the issues with speed writing?* Introduce terms: fluent, accurate, legible.
	• Use presentation to show sentence.
	• **Practice Book:** Copy the same sentence as quickly as you can.
	• **Evaluation:** *Good features of my speed writing are: Things I need to improve in my speed writing are:*
		• Settling routine
		• Use presentation to display and demonstrate the second set of words in the Practice Book.
		• **Practice Book:** Copy the words as quickly as possible; then copy them again neatly, taking extra care with letter formation and joins.
		• **Paired Talk:** Discuss the difference between the children's speed writing and their neat writing, drawing attention to letter formation, joins, angles and consistency of ascenders and descenders.
		• Use presentation to read the short passage and introduce the task.
		• **Practice Book:** Copy the passage out into their book as neatly as possible.
		• **Evaluation:** *Good features of my neat writing are: Things I need to improve in my neat writing are:*
			• Settling routine
			• **Paired Talk:** Use presentation to recap on the importance of neat handwriting and the need for speed writing at certain times.
			• **Discuss:** fluency, accuracy and legibility. *What have they learned about their own handwriting?*
			• Use presentation to read limerick and introduce task.
			• **Additional Practice sheet:** Children copy out the limerick twice, into a handwriting book or onto lined paper
			  1. neatly – timing how long it takes
			  2. speedily – timing how long it takes.
			• **Evaluation:** Compare the two versions.

Assessment criterion	Can the children: – speed write legibly and accurately when required?	– write neatly, consistently and accurately when required?	– evaluate the strengths of their handwriting and identify areas for improvement?
Further practice	Is the children's handwriting fluent, accurate and legible when writing neatly or at speed? You can ask the children to do these activities: 1. Time challenge: Write out these target words once, neatly and carefully, on lined paper, making sure the ascenders and descenders are consistent: *fluency, accuracy, legibility*. How long did it take? Write them again three more times, trying to speed up each time, without losing the accuracy and legibility. Speed challenge your friend. 2. Time challenge: Write out a verse of your favourite song as neatly as you can. Write it out again as quickly as you can. Aim to make your speed writing as accurate and legible as possible. Practice makes perfect!		

Lesson plan

Unit 2: Developing my own handwriting style and writing *f*

	Lesson 1	Lesson 2	Practice
	Class or groups seated at tables	*Class or groups seated at tables*	*Class or groups seated at tables*
Objectives	To begin to develop own fluent style of handwriting. To experiment with slanting to the right.	To continue to develop own fluent style of handwriting. Take extra care with slanting the letter *f*.	To continue to develop own fluent style of handwriting
Resources	– Practice Book Page 4 Part 1 – Presentation Part 1 – Pencil or pen	– Practice Book Page 4 Part 2 – Presentation Part 2 – Pencil or pen	– Additional Practice sheet 2 – Presentation Part 3 – Pencil or pen – Timer – Handwriting book or lined paper
Teaching	• **Settling routine and hand warm up** • Use presentation to demonstrate words containing *f*. • **Practice Book:** Copy the words. • Use presentation to discuss the quote from Mim, aged 10. • **Paired Talk:** Ask the children to discuss Mim's comments. Discuss the importance of developing a fluent and legible style of handwriting. This may include slanting but it must remain legible and retain the correct joins. • Use presentation to show sentence. • **Practice Book:** Copy the same sentence, adding a slant to their writing.	• **Settling routine** • Use presentation to demonstrate words. • Draw attention to the slant above and below the line. • Discuss the angle of the slope – a slight lean to the right can be effective, but too far and it will look like the letters are falling over. • **Practice Book:** Copy the slanting words. • Use presentation to read the facts and introduce the task. • **Practice Book:** Copy the facts, taking extra care with the formation of the letter *f*.	• **Settling routine** • **Additional Practice sheet:** Children copy the slanting letter combinations. • Use presentation to read the tongue-twister and introduce the task of completing the tongue-twister. • Ask the children to copy out the completed tongue-twister, adding a slant to the writing and taking extra care with the formation of letter *f*. • Challenge the children to say the tongue-twister three times.
Assessment criterion	**Can the children:** – experiment with developing a handwriting style by adding a slant to their writing?	– add a slant to their writing, taking extra care with the letter *f*?	– continue to develop a handwriting style, taking extra care with the letter *f*?

Further practice	Are the children beginning to develop an accurate, legible and fluent handwriting style of their own? You can ask children to do these activities:
	1. Copy out the number words, with a slanting style: *one two three four five six seven eight nine ten*
	2. Copy and illustrate this version of a traditional 'magpie' counting poem:
	   One for sorrow, two for joy, three for a girl, four for a boy.
	   Five for silver, six for gold, seven for a secret, never to be told.
	Challenge them to learn this. Can they find other verses, or other versions, of this nursery rhyme?		

Unit 3: Joining to and from *r*

	Lesson 1	**Lesson 2**	**Practice**
	Class or groups seated at tables	*Class or groups seated at tables*	*Class or groups seated at tables*
Objective	To join to and from *r*.	To practise joining to and from *r*.	To consolidate joining to and from *r*.
Resources	– Practice Book Page 5 Part 1 – Presentation Part 1 – Pencil or pen	– Practice Book Page 5 Part 2 – Presentation Part 2 – Pencil or pen	– Additional Practice sheet 3 – Presentation Part 3 – Pencil or pen – Handwriting book or lined paper
Teaching	• **Settling routine and hand warm up** • Use presentation to demonstrate joins from *r*. • **Practice Book:** Copy the same joins. • Use presentation to demonstrate words containing these joins. • Use presentation to read the jokes. Draw attention to the joins to and from the letter *r*. • **Practice Book:** Copy the same jokes.	• **Settling routine** • Use presentation to demonstrate words with joins to and from *r*. • Draw attention to the joins to and from *r*. • **Practice Book:** Copy the words. • Use presentation to read the joke. • **Practice Book:** Copy the same joke.	• **Settling routine** • **Additional Practice sheet:** Children copy letter combinations. • Use presentation to show these words: *are share shore sheer roar rare* • Time challenge: Ask the children to copy these words and time themselves. • Use presentation to introduce the task of matching the joke questions and answers, then copy them into handwriting books.
Assessment criterion	Can the children: – join to and from *r*?	– join to and from *r* consistently and accurately?	– join to and from *r* consistently and accurately in extended writing?
Further practice	Are the children's short letters formed and joined consistently in free writing? You can ask the children to do these activities: 1. Time challenge: Write these five words as many times as you can in one minute: *prepare fanfare repair improve arrive* 2. Make your own joke book. Here are three jokes to get you started: What did one plate say to another? Dinner's on me What do you call a horse that lives next door? A neighbour What do you call an alligator in a vest? An investigator		

Unit 4: Slanting key joins: diagonal joins

	Lesson 1	Lesson 2	Practice
	Class or groups seated at tables	*Class or groups seated at tables*	*Class or groups seated at tables*
Objective	To continue to develop a style of handwriting by slanting diagonal joins.	To practise slanting diagonal joins.	To consolidate slanting diagonal joins.
Resources	– Practice Book Page 6 Part 1 – Presentation Part 1 – Pencil or pen	– Practice Book Page 6 Part 2 – Presentation Part 2 – Pencil or pen	– Additional Practice sheet 4 – Presentation Part 3 – Pencil or pen – Handwriting book or lined paper
Teaching	• **Settling routine and hand warm up** • Use presentation to demonstrate the letter combinations. • Draw attention to the slant and the spacing and consistency of diagonal joins between letters. • **Practice Book:** Copy the same combinations. • Use presentation to demonstrate and discuss pairs of words containing these joins. • Use presentation to read and introduce the task of copying the passage. Draw attention to the slant, the diagonal joins and the height of t. • **Practice Book:** Copy the same passage.	• **Settling routine** • Use presentation to demonstrate words. • **Practice Book:** Copy the words. • Explain that these are adjectives but they can be turned into nouns using the suffixes –ence and –ance. • **Paired Talk:** Invite the children to think of pairs of sentences using the adjective and then the noun, for example: *The man was very intelligent.* *The intelligence of the man was evident.* • Use presentation to introduce the task of copying and completing the passage, choosing appropriate words so that it makes sense. • **Practice Book:** Copy the passage.	• **Settling routine** • **Additional Practice sheet:** Children copy the letter combinations. • Remind the children to maintain a slight slant – but not too much – and to take extra care with the spacing and consistency of the diagonal joins. • Use presentation to introduce the passage. • Ask the children to copy the passage into their handwriting books or onto lined paper.
Assessment criterion	**Can the children:** – demonstrate a slanting style of handwriting with appropriate spacing of diagonal joins?	– demonstrate a slanting style of handwriting with appropriate spacing of diagonal joins?	– demonstrate a slanting style of handwriting with appropriate spacing of diagonal joins?
Further practice	Do the children demonstrate a slanting style of handwriting in free writing, with appropriate spacing of diagonal joins? You can ask the children to do these activities: 1. Find as many words as you can ending in –ance or –ence. Give yourself one point for each word and one point for knowing the meaning. Write them out in your best handwriting. 2. Complete this newspaper report, choosing appropriate words from the list. Look up any that you are not familiar with and add them to your vocabulary. *defiant innocent incident evidence vigilant residents confident silent recent unrepentant* *Shock outcome rocks the nation. Today, Mr BB Wolf was pronounced _____. He looked _____ as he stood outside the courts but chose to remain _____ when questioned by the press. It is thought that _____ events have left the law-abiding _____ of the forest shocked and scared. They believe that the _____ at Grandma's cottage was just the beginning and they will continue to remain _____ at all times, especially when there is _____ that Wolfie is in the area.*		

Unit 5: Keeping ascenders and descenders parallel

	Lesson 1	Lesson 2	Practice
Objective	*Class or groups seated at tables* To keep ascenders and descenders constant and parallel.	*Class or groups seated at tables* To practise keeping ascenders and descenders constant and parallel.	*Class or groups seated at tables* To consolidate keeping ascenders and descenders constant and parallel.
Resources	– Practice Book Page 7 Part 1 – Presentation Part 1 – Pencil or pen	– Practice Book Page 7 Part 2 – Presentation Part 2 – Pencil or pen	– Additional Practice sheet 5 – Presentation Part 3 – Pencil or pen – Handwriting book or lined paper
Teaching	• **Settling routine and hand warm up** • Use presentation to demonstrate words. • Draw attention to the height, length and parallel consistency of the ascenders and descenders. • **Practice Book:** Copy the words. • Use presentation to demonstrate these words: *through though thought ought tough bough* • Draw attention to the height of the *t*. • Use presentation to read and introduce passage. Draw attention to the parallel ascenders and descenders. • **Practice Book:** Copy the same passage.	• **Settling routine** • Use presentation to demonstrate words. • **Practice Book:** Copy the words. • **Paired Talk:** Discuss using the suffix –*ly* to change how the word can be used in a sentence. For example: *The monkey was adorable.* *The monkey was adorably fluffy.* Ask the children to think of other examples. • Use presentation to introduce the facts about the rainforest. • **Practice Book:** Copy the passage.	• **Settling routine** • **Additional Practice sheet:** Children copy the letter combinations. • Remind the children to maintain a slight slant – but not too much – and to take extra care with the spacing and consistency of the diagonal joins. • Use presentation to introduce poem. • Ask the children to copy this poem into handwriting books or onto lined paper.
Assessment criterion	Can the children: – write carefully, keeping ascenders and descenders consistent and parallel?	– write carefully, keeping ascenders and descenders consistent and parallel?	– write carefully, keeping ascenders and descenders consistent and parallel?
Further practice	Do the children keep ascenders and descenders consistent and parallel in free writing? You can ask children to do these activities: 1. Make as many words as you can from the letters in these words: rainforest conservation. Give yourself one point for each word. Who can make the longest word? 2. Find some facts about endangered species in the rainforest. Design a poster, write an article or a letter to raise awareness.		

Lesson plan

Unit 6: Placing and spacing punctuation: sentence types

	Lesson 1	Lesson 2	Practice
Objective	*Class or groups seated at tables* To place and space punctuation correctly – questions and exclamations.	*Class or groups seated at tables* To place and space punctuation correctly – statements and commands.	*Class or groups seated at tables* To place and space punctuation correctly – different types of sentences: statements, questions, commands, exclamations.
Resources	– Practice Book Page 8 Part 1 – Presentation Part 1 – Pencil or pen	– Practice Book Page 8 Part 2 – Presentation Part 2 – Pencil or pen	– Additional Practice sheet 6 – Presentation Part 3 – Pencil or pen – Handwriting book or lined paper
Teaching	• **Settling routine and hand warm up** • Use presentation to demonstrate words: *What When Who Why Where* • Discuss when you might write these words with capital letters (start of a question, but What and How could also be used at the start of an exclamation). • **Practice Book:** Copy the words, with capital letters at the beginning. • Use presentation to discuss exclamations and questions. • Use presentation to read and introduce task: Ask the children to add the correct punctuation to the exclamations and questions. Draw attention to spacing of ! and ? • **Practice Book:** Copy and punctuate the same exclamations and questions.	• **Settling routine** • Use presentation to demonstrate words: *what how when who why where* • **Paired Talk:** Discuss when we might use these words without capital letters within sentences. For example: *He didn't know how to kick the ball.* (statement) *Stop when the whistle blows.* (command) • Use presentation to introduce the task: Ask children to punctuate the sentences and write 'statement' or 'command' in brackets. • **Practice Book:** Copy and punctuate the sentences.	• **Settling routine** • **Additional Practice sheet:** Children copy the words.: *statement question command exclamation* • **Paired Talk:** Discuss each type of sentence and ask the children to give examples incorporating: *when where who why what how* • Use presentation to introduce task: Ask children to punctuate the sentences and identify the sentence type in brackets. Take care with spacing around capital letters, ? and ! • Ask the children to copy these sentences into their handwriting books or onto lined paper.
Assessment criterion	– place and space punctuation correctly – questions and exclamations?	– place and space punctuation correctly – statements and commands?	– place and space punctuation correctly in different types of sentences: statements, questions, commands, exclamations?
Further practice	**Can the children:** – place and space punctuation correctly – questions and exclamations? Can the children place and space punctuation correctly in different types of sentences in free writing? You can ask the children to do these activities: 1. Write a sentence for each of these words BUT they cannot appear at the beginning of the sentence: *when where who why what how* 2. Choose your favourite sport or hobby and write a fact sheet with four sections: Introduction (statements); Key rules (commands); FAQs – Frequently asked questions and answers (questions and statements); Did you know? 'WOW' facts (exclamations).		

Unit 7: Writing quickly: words per minute

	Lesson 1	**Lesson 2**	**Practice**
	Class or groups seated at tables	*Class or groups seated at tables*	*Class or groups seated at tables*
Objective	To write quickly and accurately – words per minute.	To practise writing quickly and accurately – words per minute.	To consolidate writing quickly and accurately – words per minute.
Resources	– Practice Book Page 9 Part 1 – Presentation Part 1 – Pencil or pen – Timer	– Practice Book Page 9 Part 2 – Presentation Part 2 – Pencil or pen – Timer	– Additional Practice sheet 7 – Presentation Part 3 – Pencil or pen – Timer – Handwriting book or lined paper
Teaching	• **Settling routine and hand warm up** • Use presentation to demonstrate words. • Discuss the meaning of these words in relation to handwriting. • **Practice Book:** Copy the words. • Use presentation to show the sentence. • Discuss the importance of legibility even when you are writing quickly. • Use presentation to read and introduce task: Set the one-minute timer. Copy this passage quickly and make a mark when the timer reaches one minute. Complete the passage. • **Practice Book:** Copy the passage. • **Evaluation:** *I can write ____ readable words per minute.*	• **Settling routine** • Use presentation to demonstrate words. • **Paired Talk:** Discuss the meaning of these words. • **Practice Book:** Copy the words. • Use presentation to introduce the task: Set the one-minute timer. Copy this passage quickly and make a mark when the timer reaches one minute. Complete the passage. • **Practice Book:** Copy the passage. • **Evaluation:** *I can write ____ readable words per minute.*	• **Settling routine** • **Additional Practice sheet:** Children copy the words. • Use presentation to read the passage and introduce the task. It might help to choose suitable words before starting the timed task. Set the one-minute timer. Copy and complete this passage quickly in handwriting books and make a mark when the timer reaches one minute. Complete the passage. • **Evaluation:** *I can write ____ readable words per minute.* • Invite the children to discuss their speed writing. Is it fluent? legible? speeding up? getting neater? Does it take longer when they have to think of ideas? Can they hold the sentence in their head as they write?
Assessment criterion	Can the children: – copy quickly and accurately when timing themselves?	– copy quickly and accurately when timing themselves?	– write quickly and accurately when adding ideas of their own?
Further practice	Can the children write quickly, fluently and legibly when writing against the clock? You can ask the children to do these activities: 1. Write your name as many times as you can in one minute. Try a second time – can you beat your score? 2. Use the fantasy creature template to create your own creature. See how many words you can write in one minute. Have you heard of a _____? Not many people have. It is an extremely _____ creature that is only found in _____. It has _____ eyes, _____ teeth and skin the colour of _____. Its favourite meal is _____.		

Unit 8: Writing neatly: a formal message

Lesson plan

	Lesson 1	Lesson 2	Practice
Objective	*Class or groups seated at tables* To write neatly – a formal message.	*Class or groups seated at tables* To practise writing neatly – a formal message.	*Class or groups seated at tables* To consolidate writing neatly – a formal message.
Resources	– Practice Book Page 10 Part 1 – Presentation Part 1 – Pencil or pen	– Practice Book Page 10 Part 2 – Presentation Part 2 – Pencil or pen	– Additional Practice sheet 8 – Presentation Part 3 – Pencil or pen – Handwriting book or lined paper
Teaching	• **Settling routine and hand warm up** • Use presentation to demonstrate words: *honoured delighted excited sincerely* • **Practice Book:** Copy same words. • Discuss the meaning of any unknown words which may be used in a formal invitation/request. • **Paired Talk:** Use the presentation to discuss the scenario. • Use presentation to read and introduce task: Discuss the formal content of the letter, the vocabulary choices and the importance of creating a good impression through neatness. • **Practice Book:** Copy the passage as neatly as possible.	• **Settling routine** • Use presentation to demonstrate words: *enjoyed excellent* • **Practice Book:** Copy the words. • **Paired Talk:** Discuss the meaning of any unknown words which may be used in a formal thank you letter. Can the children suggest any synonyms? • Use presentation to read and introduce the task to write a formal thank you letter. • **Practice Book:** Copy the passage as neatly as possible.	• **Settling routine** • **Additional Practice sheet:** Children copy the words. • Use presentation to introduce task: Copy and complete the formal letter. Use appropriate words to complete the passage. • Copy the completed passage into handwriting books or onto lined paper.
Assessment criterion	Can the children: – write neatly in a formal message?	– write neatly in a formal message?	– write neatly in a formal message?
Further practice	Can the children write neatly in a formal message in free writing? You can ask the children to do these activities: 1. Write a formal letter to any person of your choice, explaining why you admire them, thanking them for what they do or requesting advice. 2. Turn this invitation into a more formal message and write it in your best handwriting, setting it out neatly on the page: *Hi Non. I'm having a b'day party. It's on Sat, June 6th. 4–7pm. It'd be great if you could come. Let me know. See you.*		

Happy Handwriting

Lesson plan

Unit 9: Writing brief notes about an event

	Lesson 1	Lesson 2	Practice
	Class or groups seated at tables	*Class or groups seated at tables*	*Class or groups seated at tables*
Objective	To write brief notes about an event.	To turn brief notes into a recount.	To turn brief notes into a recount.
Resources	– Practice Book Page 11 Part 1 – Presentation Part 1 – Pencil or pen	– Practice Book Page 11 Part 2 – Presentation Part 2 – Pencil or pen	– Additional Practice sheet 9 – Presentation Part 3 – Pencil or pen – Handwriting book or lined paper
Teaching	• **Settling routine and hand warm up** • Use presentation to demonstrate joins. • **Practice Book:** Copy same joins. • Use presentation to show image. • **Paired Talk:** Ask the children to discuss the image. What questions would they be asking if they were reporting on the incident? • Take feedback, then reveal the brief notes. • **Practice Book:** Copy the notes as quickly as possible but the notes must still be legible.	• **Settling routine** • Use presentation to demonstrate words. • **Practice Book:** Copy the words. • **Paired Talk:** Discuss the notes from the previous lesson. Use them to deliver a TV-style report. • Use presentation to read and introduce the update for a local news website. • **Practice Book:** Copy the passage as neatly as possible and then compare writing with brief notes from previous lesson.	• **Settling routine** • **Additional Practice sheet:** Children copy the words quickly. • Use presentation to introduce task: Copy and complete the update on the event for the local news website. • Copy the passage neatly into handwriting books or onto lined paper
Assessment criterion	Can the children: – write speedily but legibly when making brief notes?	– write neatly and accurately when necessary?	– write both speedily but legibly when required, and neatly and accurately when necessary?
Further practice	Can the children make brief notes quickly but accurately when required in free writing? You can ask the children to do these activities: 1. Speed challenge: Be an estate agent and describe your house, or your dream house, in note form. Decide what information is important. You have five minutes! 2. Imagine you are a reporter and have been asked to write something for a local news website. Make brief notes to jog your memory so that you would be able to write them up later. Choose anything you are familiar with, such as a sporting event; a school play; a film you have watched; a new game; a book; a local place; or an imaginary event.		

Happy Handwriting

Unit 10: Self-assessment

Lesson plan

	Lesson 1	Lesson 2	Practice
Objectives	*Class or groups seated at tables* To assess joining to and from r; placing and spacing of capital letters and end punctuation; tall letters.	*Class or groups seated at tables* To assess legibility and fluency of speed writing.	*Class or groups seated at tables* To assess the quality, accuracy and style of my neat writing, recognise improvements and plan next steps.
Resources	– Practice Book Page 12 Part 1 – Presentation Part 1 – Pencil or pen	– Practice Book Page 12 Part 2 – Presentation Part 2 – Pencil or pen – Timer	– Presentation Part 3 – Pencil or pen – Handwriting book or lined paper
Teaching	• **Settling routine** • Use presentation to discuss the two sentences. • Draw attention to: the two different sentence types; joining to and from r; placing and spacing of capital letters and end punctuation; tall letters. • Use presentation to introduce task. • **Practice Book:** Copy the passage. • Use presentation to introduce assessment. Ask children to assess the consistency of their joins to and from r; the placing and spacing of capital letters and end punctuation; consistency and angle of tall letters.	• **Settling routine** • Use presentation to introduce the passage and task. Set the timer. Copy this description as quickly as you can. Make a mark after one minute, then complete the passage. • **Practice Book:** Copy the passage. • Use presentation to introduce assessment: Ask children to assess the legibility of their speed writing and record the number of words per minute.	• **Settling routine** • Use presentation to introduce activity. Children to copy the poem as neatly as possible, focusing on style and appearance, then copy and complete the self-assessment sentences. • Use presentation to introduce evaluation and next steps: *This term, I have improved at …* *I need to practise …*
Assessment criterion	**Can the children:** – evaluate their handwriting accurately when focusing on: joining to and from r; placing and spacing of capital letters and end punctuation; tall letters?	– assess their handwriting accurately when focusing on: legibility and fluency of speed writing?	– assess their handwriting accurately when focusing on: the quality, accuracy and style of their neat writing? – recognise improvements and plan next steps?
Further practice	Do the children need more handwriting practice in free writing? You can ask the children to do these activities: 1. Write a verse from your favourite festive song and illustrate it. 2. Make a card for a special person and find a suitable poem to write inside.		

Unit 11: Spacing key joins: horizontal joins

	Lesson 1	Lesson 2	Practice
	Class or groups seated at tables	*Class or groups seated at tables*	*Class or groups seated at tables*
Objective	To focus on spacing key joins: horizontal joins to and from *o v w*.	To practise spacing key joins: horizontal joins from *r* and to and from *o*.	To consolidate spacing key joins – horizontal joins.
Resources	– Practice Book Page 13 Part 1 – Presentation Part 1 – Pencil or pen	– Practice Book Page 13 Part 2 – Presentation Part 2 – Pencil or pen	– Additional Practice sheet 11 – Presentation Part 3 – Pencil or pen – Handwriting book or lined paper
Teaching	• Settling routine and hand warm up • Use presentation to demonstrate the prefixes. • **Practice Book:** Copy the same prefixes, taking care with horizontal joins to and from *o, v* and *w*. • Remind the children that many words are made up of a root word and affixes. • Use presentation to demonstrate and discuss meanings of words containing the prefixes. • Use presentation to read and introduce the sentence completion task. • **Practice Book:** Complete and copy the same sentence.	• Settling routine • Use presentation to demonstrate words. • Draw attention to the joins to and from *r* and discuss the two homonyms (meaning notepaper/still). • **Practice Book:** Copy the words. • Use presentation to read the recipe instructions. • **Practice Book:** Copy the instructions.	• Settling routine • **Additional Practice sheet:** Children copy the prefixes. • Draw attention to the horizontal joins and discuss meaning of prefixes. • Use presentation to introduce task and discuss which words to choose to complete the restaurant review. • Copy the completed passage into handwriting books or onto lined paper.
Assessment criterion	Can the children: – space key horizontal joins accurately: joins to and from *o v w*?	– space key horizontal joins accurately: joins from *r* and to and from *o*?	– space key horizontal joins accurately?
Further practice	Do the children space horizontal joins accurately in free writing? You can ask the children to do these activities: 1. Copy out a recipe for your favourite dish, then make it (with permission of course)! 2. Find as many words as you can with the prefixes: under, over, auto, micro, inter. Can you work out what they all mean?		

Lesson plan

Unit 12: Joining and breaking for descenders

	Lesson 1	Lesson 2	Practice
Objective	*Class or groups seated at tables* To focus on joins and breaks to and from descenders.	*Class or groups seated at tables* To practise joins and breaks to and from descenders.	*Class or groups seated at tables* To consolidate joins and breaks to and from descenders.
Resources	– Practice Book Page 14 Part 1 – Presentation Part 1 – Pencil or pen	– Practice Book Page 14 Part 2 – Presentation Part 2 – Pencil or pen	– Additional Practice sheet 12 – Presentation Part 3 – Pencil or pen – Handwriting book or lined paper
Teaching	• **Settling routine and hand warm up** • Use presentation to demonstrate words. • **Practice Book:** Copy the words, taking care with descenders. • Remind the children that descenders usually join to but not from *j g y p q* . Only *f* joins to and from. • Use presentation to demonstrate this. • Use presentation to read and introduce task of copying the safety tips. • **Practice Book:** Copy the same safety tips.	• **Settling routine** • Use presentation to demonstrate words. • Draw attention to the joins to and breaks from descenders, apart from the letter *f*. • **Practice Book:** Copy the words. • Use presentation to read the poem. • **Practice Book:** Copy the poem, taking extra care with joins to and breaks from descenders.	• **Settling routine** • **Additional Practice sheet:** Children copy the words. • **Paired Talk:** Invite students to use the presentation to read a weather forecast, in the style of a TV weather person. • Copy out the weather forecast into handwriting books or onto lined paper.
Assessment criterion	– demonstrate appropriate joins and breaks to and from descenders?	– demonstrate appropriate joins and breaks to and from descenders?	– demonstrate appropriate joins and breaks to and from descenders?
Further practice	**Can the children:** Are the children making appropriate joins and breaks to and from descenders in free writing? You can ask the children to do these activities: 1. Copy out these weather words and design a weather chart symbol for each one: *sunny blustery showery wintery foggy bright stormy*. 2. Copy and illustrate these traditional rhymes about the weather. Can you find any others? *Red sky at night, shepherd's delight. Red sky in the morning, shepherd's warning.* *Evening red and morning grey will set a voyager on his way. But evening grey and morning red will bring down rain upon his head.*		

28   Happy Handwriting

Unit 13: Writing words with qu

	Lesson 1	Lesson 2	Practice
Objective	*Class or groups seated at tables* To write words with *qu*.	*Class or groups seated at tables* To practise writing words with *qu*.	*Class or groups seated at tables* To consolidate writing words with *qu*.
Resources	– Practice Book Page 15 Part 1 – Presentation Part 1 – Pencil or pen	– Practice Book Page 15 Part 2 – Presentation Part 2 – Pencil or pen	– Additional Practice sheet 13 – Presentation Part 3 – Pencil or pen – Handwriting book or lined paper
Teaching	• **Settling routine and hand warm up** • Use presentation to demonstrate combinations with *qu*. • Draw attention to the fact that you can join to *q* but not from it. • **Practice Book:** Copy the same joins. • Use presentation to demonstrate words containing the combinations. • Use presentation to introduce task of completing, then copying the passage. • **Practice Book:** Complete and copy the same passage.	• **Settling routine** • Use presentation to demonstrate words. • Draw attention to the fact that although *q* and *u* always go together as a team, they don't join. • **Practice Book:** Copy the words. • Use presentation to read passage and introduce task to copy the information as neatly as possible. • **Practice Book:** Copy the same passage in their neatest handwriting.	• **Settling routine** • **Additional Practice sheet:** Children copy the words. • Use presentation to read and complete the poem. • Copy the completed poem into handwriting books or onto lined paper.
Assessment criterion	Can the children: – write words containing *qu*?	– join to *q* when writing *qu* words?	– write words containing *qu* accurately in extended writing?

Further practice	Can the children write words containing *qu* accurately in free writing? You can ask the children to do these activities:
	1. Challenge: How many words can you make from these letters? q u e a i o s t l t
	2. Copy these tongue-twisters and say them three times:
	    It's quite quiet in the queue, but queues are often quite quiet.
	    The quarrelsome queen frequently quarrelled.
	    The noisy duck was quick to quack but when the quiet duck quacked it wasn't always quick.		

Unit 14: Placing and spacing punctuation: apostrophes in contractions

	Lesson 1	**Lesson 2**	**Practice**
	Class or groups seated at tables	*Class or groups seated at tables*	*Class or groups seated at tables*
Objective	To place and space apostrophes in contractions.	To practise placing and spacing apostrophes in contractions.	To consolidate placing and spacing apostrophes in contractions.
Resources	– Practice Book Page 16 Part 1 – Presentation Part 1 – Pencil or pen	– Practice Book Page 16 Part 2 – Presentation Part 2 – Pencil or pen	– Additional Practice sheet 14 – Presentation Part 3 – Pencil or pen – Handwriting book or lined paper

Teaching	• **Settling routine and hand warm up**
	• Use presentation to demonstrate contractions.
	• Discuss contractions and draw attention to the placing and spacing of the apostrophes.
	• **Practice Book:** Copy the same contractions.
	• Use presentation to demonstrate and discuss other contractions.
	  Remind students that it is *might have*, not *might of*.
	• Use presentation to read and introduce task of completing the diary entry.
	• **Practice Book:** Complete and copy the same diary entry.
		• **Settling routine**
		• Use presentation to demonstrate words.
		• **Practice Book:** Copy the words. Explain that these are negative contractions.
		• Discuss *will not – won't*
		• **Paired Talk:** Invite the children to give examples of making sentences negative, using contractions:
		  He is feeling tired. (*He isn't feeling tired.*)
		  He did want to go. (*He didn't want to go.*)
		• Use presentation to introduce the task: Turn the diary entry into a negative one.
		• **Practice Book:** Copy the passage, adding negative contractions.
			• **Settling routine**
			• **Additional Practice sheet:** Children copy the contractions.
			  Discuss the placing and spacing of the apostrophes.
			• Use presentation to introduce task: Make the diary entry 'chattier' and more informal by using contractions for the words underlined.
			• Copy this passage into handwriting books or onto lined paper.

Assessment criterion	**Can the children:** – place and space apostrophes in contractions?	– place and space apostrophes in negative contractions?	– place and space apostrophes in contractions in informal writing?
Further practice	Do the children place and space apostrophes in contractions in free writing? You can ask the children to do these activities: 1. List as many contractions as you can. How many can you find? 2. Copy out the lyrics to a song or a favourite pop song, removing all the contractions and writing the words out in full. Try singing the song. It sounds very strange, and it can be hard to fit all the words in! For example: *She will be coming round the mountain when she comes.*		

Unit 15: Getting the height right: capital letters

	Lesson	Lesson 2	Practice
	Class or groups seated at tables	*Class or groups seated at tables*	*Class or groups seated at tables*
Objective	To focus on getting the height right: capital letters.	To practise getting the height right: capital letters.	To consolidate getting the height right: capital letters.
Resources	– Practice Book Page 17 Part 1 – Presentation Part 1 – Pencil or pen	– Practice Book Page 17 Part 2 – Presentation Part 2 – Pencil or pen	– Additional Practice sheet 15 – Presentation Part 3 – Pencil or pen – Handwriting book or lined paper
Teaching	• **Settling routine and hand warm up** • Use presentation to demonstrate all capital letters of the alphabet: A–Z. • **Practice Book:** Copy the capital letters. • Use presentation to demonstrate the sentence. • Draw attention to the height of the capital letters – slightly shorter than tall letters, but taller than t. • Use presentation to read and introduce task: Copy the information, taking extra care with the height of the capital letters. • **Practice Book:** Copy the same passage, taking care to ensure capital letters are the correct height.	• **Settling routine** • Use presentation to demonstrate words. • **Practice Book:** Copy the words. • **Paired Talk:** Discuss the use of capital letters and draw attention to the relative height of the letters. • Use presentation to introduce the task: Copy the information, taking care with the height of tall letters and capital letters. • **Practice Book:** Copy the same passage.	• **Settling routine** • **Additional Practice sheet:** Children copy the initials. • **Paired Talk:** What do you think the initials stand for? • Use presentation to introduce task: Read and copy the global poem. Find the places in an atlas. • Copy the poem into handwriting books or onto lined paper.
Assessment criterion	**Can the children:** – write capital letters accurately, getting the height right?	– write capital letters accurately, getting the height right?	– write capital letters accurately, getting the height right?
Further practice	Do the children write capital letters accurately, getting the height right in free writing? You can ask the children to do these activities: 1. Write the days of the week and the months of the year, focusing on the relative height of the tall letters and capital letters. 2. Try writing another verse for the poem about travelling the world. Use the index of an atlas to help you.		

Lesson plan

Unit 16: Placing and spacing punctuation: commas and semi-colons

	Lesson 1	Lesson 2	Practice
	Class or groups seated at tables	*Class or groups seated at tables*	*Class or groups seated at tables*
Objective	To place and space punctuation correctly: commas before coordinating conjunctions.	To place and space punctuation correctly: semi-colons separating two independent clauses.	To place and space punctuation correctly: commas in a list.
Resources	– Practice Book Page 18 Part 1 – Presentation Part 1 – Pencil or pen	– Practice Book Page 18 Part 2 – Presentation Part 2 – Pencil or pen	– Additional Practice sheet 16 – Presentation Part 3 – Pencil or pen – Handwriting book or lined paper
Teaching	• **Settling routine and hand warm up** • Use presentation to demonstrate words. • **Paired Talk:** Discuss coordinating conjunctions used to separate two independent clauses. • **Practice Book:** Copy the words. • Use presentation to discuss the spacing of commas before coordinating conjunctions. There should be a space after the comma. • Use presentation to read and introduce task: Copy the online review, taking care with the spacing. • **Practice Book:** Copy the online review.	• **Settling routine** • Use presentation to demonstrate words. • **Practice Book:** Copy the words and punctuation marks. • **Paired Talk:** Discuss when we might use these items of punctuation. • Remind the children that the semi-colon can be used to separate two independent (main) clauses that are closely related, for example: *It was hot; the sun was beating down.* Draw attention to the spacing after the semi-colon. • Use presentation to introduce the task: Space the sentences correctly. • **Practice Book:** Copy the sentences, spacing the words correctly.	• **Settling routine** • **Additional Practice sheet:** Children to copy the sentence. • **Paired Talk:** Discuss the use of commas in a list and focus on the spacing after the comma. • Use presentation to introduce task: Punctuate and space the online review correctly. • Copy the passage into handwriting books or onto lined paper.
Assessment criterion	**Can the children:** – place and space punctuation correctly – commas before coordinating conjunctions?	– place and space punctuation correctly – semi-colons separating two independent clauses?	– place and space punctuation – commas in a list?
Further practice	Can the children place and space commas and semi-colons correctly in free writing? You can ask the children to do these activities: 1. Write a second independent clause to finish these sentences: *I like swimming; I bought a tennis racquet; They didn't have it in red;* 2. Write five sentences about something you are interested in such as a hobby, a sport, a pop star or a place. Each sentence MUST include at least two commas in a list. For example: *You will need a swimming costume, a mask, a snorkel and some flippers. You can snorkel in pools, lakes, rivers and the sea.*		

Happy Handwriting

Unit 17: Writing quickly: making notes

	Lesson 1	Lesson 2	Practice
	Class or groups seated at tables	*Class or groups seated at tables*	*Class or groups seated at tables*
Objective	To write quickly and accurately – making notes.	To practise writing quickly and accurately – making notes.	To consolidate writing quickly and accurately – making notes.
Resources	– Practice Book Page 19 Part 1 – Presentation Part 1 – Pencil or pencil – Timer	– Practice Book Page 19 Part 2 – Presentation Part 2 – Pencil or pencil – Timer	– Additional Practice sheet 17 – Presentation Part 3 – Pencil or pencil – Timer – Handwriting book or lined paper
Teaching	• Settling routine and hand warm up • Use presentation to demonstrate words. • **Practice Book:** Copy the words. • Use presentation to show the definition. • Use presentation to show the full directions to the skateboard park with the key information underlined, and introduce task: Can you make notes of the key points in one minute? • **Practice Book:** Write down the key information in note form as quickly as you can. Ask: *Is it legible? Can you retell the information using your notes?*	• Settling routine • Use presentation to demonstrate words. • **Paired Talk:** Discuss the meaning of these words. • **Practice Book:** Copy the words. • Use presentation to read the passage and agree key information. • **Practice Book:** Ask the children to write the key information in note form as quickly as they can. Use their notes to retell the information to a friend.	• Settling routine • **Additional Practice sheet:** Children copy the words. • Use presentation to read the passage and introduce the task: Underline key information/words. Set the timer and write notes as quickly as they can. • Use their notes to retell the information to a friend.
Assessment criterion	**Can the children:** – write notes quickly, accurately and legibly when timing themselves?	– identify key information and write notes quickly, accurately and legibly when timing themselves?	– identify key information and write notes quickly, accurately and legibly when timing themselves?
Further practice	Can the children write notes quickly, fluently and legibly when writing against the clock? You can ask the children to do these activities: 1. Find a piece of information about something you are interested in. Underline key words and phrases and write your notes as quickly as you can. 2. Watch a programme, video or film about something you're interested in and make notes using key words and phrases. Use your notes to tell your friends about it.		

Unit 18: Writing neatly and printing

	Lesson 1	Lesson 2	Practice
Objective	*Class or groups seated at tables* To write neatly and print: labels.	*Class or groups seated at tables* To write neatly and print: for younger readers.	*Class or groups seated at tables* To write neatly and print: posters.
Resources	– Practice Book Page 20 Part 1 – Presentation Part 1 – Pencil	– Practice Book Page 20 Part 2 – Presentation Part 2 – Pencil	– Additional Practice sheet 18 – Presentation Part 3 – Pencil – Handwriting book or lined paper
Teaching	• **Settling routine and hand warm up** • Use presentation to demonstrate words. • **Practice Book:** Copy same words. • **Paired Talk:** Use presentation to discuss the questions: *What is meant by printing as opposed to joining? When might it be necessary to print rather than join?* For example: when filling in a form; labelling a diagram/map; writing something for a younger person to read. • Use presentation to introduce task and discuss the labelling of the map. • **Practice Book:** Copy the labels, printing neatly.	• **Settling routine** • Use presentation to demonstrate words. • **Practice Book:** Copy the words. • **Paired Talk:** Discuss the meaning of any unknown words. Ask the children why it might be necessary to print neatly for younger readers. • Use presentation to read the passage and introduce the task. • **Practice Book:** Copy the passage, printing as neatly as possible so that it can be read by younger readers.	• **Settling routine** • **Additional Practice sheet:** Children copy the words. • Use presentation to introduce the task: Create a poster to advertise something to the public, or provide information. • Copy the poster into handwriting books or onto lined paper.
Assessment criterion	Can the children: – write neatly when labelling a map?	– write neatly for younger readers?	– write neatly in a formal poster?
Further practice	Can the children write neatly and print when required in free writing? You can ask the children to do these activities: 1. Make a poster advertising an event of your choice, or giving information about an important issue, such as climate change, conservation or road safety. 2. Make a book for a younger child and illustrate it. Copy out a story or rhyme, or make up your own. Remember to print neatly so they can read it for themselves. Wrap it up and give it to them as a present.		

Unit 19: Alphabetical order: advanced

	Lesson 1	Lesson 2	Practice
	Class or groups seated at tables	*Class or groups seated at tables*	*Class or groups seated at tables*
Objective	To revise writing alphabetical order to the second and third letter.	To practise writing alphabetical order to the second, third and fourth letter.	To practise writing alphabetical order – further letters.
Resources	– Practice Book Page 21 Part 1 – Presentation Part 1 – Pencil or pen	– Practice Book Page 21 Part 2 – Presentation Part 2 – Pencil	– Additional Practice sheet 19 – Presentation Part 3 – Pencil – Handwriting book or lined paper
Teaching	• Settling routine and hand warm up • Use presentation to demonstrate joins. • **Practice Book:** Copy the words, then put them into alphabetical order. • **Paired Talk: Discuss:** *What happens if the first letter is the same? What happens if the first and second letters are the same?* • Use presentation to introduce task: Write out the alphabet, then list the categories in alphabetical order. • **Practice Book:** List the categories in alphabetical order, taking care to join handwriting accurately and neatly.	• Settling routine • Use presentation to demonstrate words. • **Practice Book:** Copy the words. • **Paired Talk: Discuss:** *When or where might you find things/people/information arranged in alphabetical order?* (For example: register; index; library) • Use presentation to introduce the task of arranging the classic book titles in alphabetical order. • **Practice Book:** Rearrange these classic book titles in alphabetical order.	• Settling routine • **Additional Practice sheet:** Children copy the words quickly. • Explain: *In libraries, fiction is often arranged in alphabetical order by author, surnames first. If two or more authors have the same surname, the usual alphabetical order rules are applied to their first names.* • Use presentation to introduce task: Reorder the "W" shelf of authors, surnames first. • Ask the children to arrange the authors into alphabetical order, surnames first, then copy this list neatly into handwriting books or onto lined paper.
Assessment criterion	Can the children: – write in alphabetical order to the second and third letter?	– write in alphabetical order to the second, third and fourth letter?	– write in alphabetical order when required?
Further practice	Can the children apply the rules of alphabetical order when required? You can ask the children to do these activities: 1. Write down five books you have enjoyed. Arrange them in alphabetical order by authors, surname first. 2. Visit the library. On the fiction shelves, choose a letter and write down the surnames of 20 or more authors.		

Unit 20: Self-assessment

	Lesson 1	Lesson 2	Practice
	Class or groups seated at tables	*Class or groups seated at tables*	*Class or groups seated at tables*
Objective	To assess: horizontal joins from *o*, *v* and *w*; spacing of commas and semi-colons within sentences; the height of capital letters.	To assess: legibility, accuracy and fluency of speed writing.	To assess the quality, accuracy and style of my neat writing, recognise improvements and plan next steps.
Resources	– Practice Book Page 22 Part 1 – Presentation Part 1 – Pencil or pen	– Practice Book Page 22 Part 2 – Presentation Part 2 – Pencil or pen – Timer	– Presentation Part 3 – Pencil – Handwriting book or lined paper
Teaching	• **Settling routine** • Use presentation to discuss these two sentences. *In spring, colourful flowers fill gardens and hedgerows. I like all spring flowers, but I love daffodils the most.* Draw attention to: horizontal joins from *o*, *v* and *w*; spacing of commas within sentences; the height of the capital letters. • Use presentation to read the passage and introduce task. • **Practice Book:** Copy the passage neatly. • Use presentation to introduce assessment: Ask the children to assess the consistency of their horizontal joins from *o*, *v* and *w*; spacing of commas and semi-colons within sentences; the height of the capital letters.	• **Settling routine** • Use presentation to introduce task: Set the timer. Copy this information as quickly as possible. Make a mark after one minute, then complete the passage. • **Practice Book:** Copy passage. • Use presentation to introduce assessment: Ask children to assess the legibility of their speed writing and record the number of words per minute.	• **Settling routine** • Use presentation to read the poem. Ask: *Who is 'she'?* (Spring). Ask the children to copy this poem as neatly as possible, focusing on style and appearance, then complete the self-assessment sentences. • Use presentation to introduce evaluation and next steps: *This term, I have improved at …* *I need to practise …*
Assessment criterion	**Can the children:** – evaluate their handwriting accurately when focusing on: horizontal joins from *o*, *v* and *w*; spacing of commas and semi-colons within sentences; the height of capital letters?	– assess their handwriting accurately when focusing on: legibility and fluency of speed writing?	– assess their handwriting accurately when focusing on: the quality, accuracy and style of their neat writing? – recognise improvements and plan next steps?
Further practice	Do the children need more handwriting practice in free writing? You can ask the children to do these activities: 1. Write a verse from your favourite seasonal song and illustrate it. 2. Make a card for a special person and find a suitable spring poem to write inside. Or better still – write one yourself.		

Unit 21: Spacing key joins: practising spacing and using compound words

	Lesson 1	Lesson 2	Practice
	Class or groups seated at tables	*Class or groups seated at tables*	*Class or groups seated at tables*
Objective	To focus on spacing and using compound words.	To practise spacing and using compound words.	To consolidate spacing and using compound words.
Resources	– Practice Book Page 23 Part 1 – Presentation Part 1 – Pencil or pen	– Practice Book Page 23 Part 2 – Presentation Part 2 – Pencil or pen	– Additional Practice sheet 21 – Presentation Part 3 – Pencil or pen – Handwriting book or lined paper
Teaching	• **Settling routine and hand warm up** • Use presentation to demonstrate words. • **Practice Book:** Copy the words. • Remind the children that some nouns are made up of two nouns joined together – compound words. • Use presentation to demonstrate and discuss meanings of the compound words. • Use presentation to read and introduce task: Make ten compound words using the words given. Write them out neatly. Ask children to notice where they take their pen off the paper. • **Practice Book:** Make ten compound words using the given words.	• **Settling routine** • Use presentation to demonstrate compound words. • **Practice Book:** Copy the words. • Explain that some compound words are hyphenated. These can sometimes act as adjectives, for example: *razor-sharp cold-hearted part-time* • **Paired Talk:** Ask the children to think of other compound words that act as an adjective. • Use presentation to reintroduce the task: Read the definitions and choose the hyphenated compound word that matches each definition. Note the spacing of the hyphen. Copy the definitions and hyphenated compound words neatly. • **Practice Book:** Copy the definitions and the hyphenated compound words.	• **Settling routine** • Use presentation to demonstrate words. • **Additional Practice sheet:** Children copy the words. • Discuss the spacing of hyphens. Explain that writers often use hyphenated adjectives to make the writing less wordy and clumsy, for example: *race run at a very fast pace – fast-paced race* • Use presentation to introduce task: Play 'Hyphen or No Hyphen?'. Decide whether the compound words should have a hyphen or no hyphen. • Copy the passage into handwriting books or onto lined paper, adding hyphens where needed.
Assessment criterion	Can the children: – space compound words correctly – without hyphens?	– space compound words correctly – with hyphens?	– space compound words correctly – with and without hyphens in a passage?
Further practice	Do the children space compound words correctly in free writing? You can ask the children to do these activities: 1. Make as many compound words as you can starting with: *black, bed* and *sun* 2. Using as many compound words as you can, describe some people or things that you like, for example: mouse – *long tailed*; *bright-eyed*; *twitchy-nosed*.		

Unit 22: Slanting your writing

Lesson plan

	Lesson 1	Lesson 2	Practice
Objective	*Class or groups seated at tables* To focus on slanting your writing.	*Class or groups seated at tables* To practise slanting your writing.	*Class or groups seated at tables* To consolidate slanting your writing.
Resources	– Practice Book Page 24 Part 1 – Presentation Part 1 – Pencil or pen	– Practice Book Page 24 Part 2 – Presentation Part 2 – Pencil or pen	– Additional Practice sheet 22 – Presentation Part 3 – Pencil or pen – Handwriting book or lined paper
Teaching	• **Settling routine and hand warm up** • Use presentation to demonstrate words. • **Practice Book:** Copy the words. • Use presentation to demonstrate slanting writing. • **Paired Talk:** Discuss when you might write a neat handwritten piece – letter, card, instructions, display. • Use presentation to read and introduce task: Use slanted writing to copy the passage. • **Practice Book:** Copy the same handwritten note, slanting their writing to the right.	• **Settling routine** • Use presentation to demonstrate words. • Draw attention to the slanted style. • **Practice Book:** Copy the words, taking care with the style. • Use presentation to read the agenda for the meeting and introduce the task. • **Practice Book:** Copy the agenda, taking extra care with slanting of writing.	• **Settling routine** • Use presentation to demonstrate words. • **Additional Practice sheet:** Children copy the words. • Use presentation to read the appeal and introduce the task. • Copy the note into handwriting books or onto lined paper.
Assessment criterion	Can the children: – develop a personal style by slanting their writing?	– develop a personal style by slanting their writing?	– develop a personal style by slanting their writing?
Further practice	Are the children developing a personal style by slanting their writing in free writing? You can ask the children to do these activities: 1. Write a neat card or note to a friend or family member, for example: thanking them for doing something; wishing them good luck; passing on some information. 2. Choose a short poem that you like and write it out neatly for the wall. Remember to slant your writing and give it some style.		

Unit 23: Revising key joins: joins to round letters

	Lesson 1	Lesson 2	Practice
	Class or groups seated at tables	*Class or groups seated at tables*	*Class or groups seated at tables*
Objective	To join round letters accurately: *c a d q*.	To join round letters accurately: *o g c a d*.	To join round letters accurately and break after *p* and *g*.
Resources	– Practice Book Page 25 Part 1 – Presentation Part 1 – Pencil or pen	– Practice Book Page 25 Part 2 – Presentation Part 2 – Pencil or pen	– Additional Practice sheet 23 – Presentation Part 3 – Pencil or pen – Handwriting book or lined paper
Teaching	• **Settling routine and hand warm up** • Use presentation to demonstrate words. • **Practice Book:** Copy the words. • Use presentation to demonstrate these words: *decide decided deciding decider* • **Paired Talk:** Discuss the word endings and put them into sentences. • Use presentation to introduce task: Discuss the meaning of these words, then complete and copy the sentences. • **Practice Book:** Complete and copy the sentences.	• **Settling routine** • Use presentation to demonstrate words. • Draw attention to the joins around *o g c a d* and the sharp change in direction when forming the letters. • **Practice Book:** Copy the words. • Use presentation to read the match report. • **Practice Book:** Copy the blog in their neatest joined handwriting.	• **Settling routine** • Use presentation to demonstrate the words. • Draw attention to joins to and from round letters and highlight the break letters *p* and *g*. • **Additional Practice sheet:** Children copy the words. • Use presentation to read the poem and introduce task. • Copy this poem into handwriting books or onto lined paper.
Assessment criterion	Can the children: – join round letters accurately: *c a d q*?	– join round letters accurately: *o g c a d*?	– join round letters accurately and break after *p* and *g*?
Further practice	Can the children join round letters accurately in free writing? You can ask the children to do these activities: 1. Challenge: How many words, of four letters or more, can you make from these letters: *c d g p q b a e i o u* 2. Design a persuasive advert to attract new players to join the Regal Tennis Club. You could include phrases such as: *Improve your health; Meet new people; Beginners welcome; Come along; No experience necessary; Don't delay – join today!*		

Unit 24: Spacing tricky joins

Lesson plan

	Lesson 1	Lesson 2	Practice
	Class or groups seated at tables	*Class or groups seated at tables*	*Class or groups seated at tables*
Objective	To write words with f and r accurately.	To practise writing words with f and r accurately.	To consolidate writing words with f and r accurately.
Resources	– Practice Book Page 26 Part 1 – Presentation Part 1 – Pencil or pen	– Practice Book Page 26 Part 2 – Presentation Part 2 – Pencil or pen	– Additional Practice sheet 24 – Presentation Part 3 – Pencil or pen – Handwriting book or lined paper
Teaching	• **Settling routine and hand warm up** • Use presentation to demonstrate combinations. • Draw attention to joins to and from f and r. • **Practice Book:** Copy the words. • Use presentation to demonstrate these words and discuss the past tense spelling: *prefer/preferred transfer/transferred* • Use presentation to introduce task: Discuss the meaning of these words, then complete and copy the passage. • **Practice Book:** Complete and copy the same passage.	• **Settling routine** • Use presentation to demonstrate words. • Draw attention to the joins around f and r. • **Practice Book:** Copy the words. • Use presentation to read the advertisement. • **Practice Book:** Copy the advertisement in their neatest handwriting.	• **Settling routine** • Use presentation to demonstrate words. • **Additional Practice sheet:** Children copy the words. • Use presentation to read the reference and introduce task. • Copy and complete the reference into handwriting books or onto lined paper.
Assessment criterion	Can the children: – write words with f and r accurately?	– write words with f and r accurately?	– write words with f and r accurately?
Further practice	Do the children write words with f and r accurately in free writing? You can ask the children to do these activities: 1. Make a list of things you are looking forward to doing in school next year. 2. Write an advert for your current school. What are its strengths? What would attract new children to come to your school?		

Unit 25: Proofreading and paragraphing

	Lesson 1	Lesson 2	Practice
	Class or groups seated at tables	*Class or groups seated at tables*	*Class or groups seated at tables*
Objective	To improve proofreading skills.	To focus on paragraphing.	To improve proofreading skills and focus on paragraphing.
Resources	– Practice Book Page 27 Part 1 – Presentation Part 1 – Pencil or pen	– Practice Book Page 27 Part 2 – Presentation Part 2 – Pencil or pen	– Additional Practice sheet 25 – Presentation Part 3 – Pencil or pen – Handwriting book or lined paper
Teaching	• **Settling routine and hand warm up** • Use presentation to demonstrate words. • **Practice Book:** Copy the words. • Use presentation to demonstrate the sentence and discuss the mistakes: *why do peeple leave there rubish on the beech.* (*Why do people leave their rubbish on the beach?*) • Use presentation to introduce task: Proofread the handwritten letter extract, correct it and write it out neatly. • **Practice Book:** Correct same passage and copy.	• **Settling routine** • Use presentation to demonstrate words. • **Practice Book:** Copy the words. • **Paired Talk:** Remind each other when you might need a new paragraph in writing. • Use presentation to read the passage. Identify the two themes and underline the sentences in two different colours. Rewrite as two paragraphs. • **Practice Book:** Copy the information as two paragraphs in their neatest handwriting.	• **Settling routine** • Use presentation to demonstrate words. • **Additional Practice sheet:** Children copy the words. Proofread and rewrite the biography, separated into paragraphs. • Use presentation to introduce task. Proofread and rewrite the biography, separated into paragraphs. • Copy the biography, with paragraphs, into handwriting books or onto lined paper.
Assessment criterion	Can the children: – proofread and correct mistakes, rewriting neatly?	– rewrite neatly, organising information into paragraphs?	– proofread, then rewrite neatly, organising information into paragraphs?
Further practice	Do the children proofread, then rewrite neatly, organising information into paragraphs in free writing? You can ask the children to do these activities: 1. Help to reduce plastic waste by writing a letter to a company of your choice. Use three paragraphs: 1. introduction/background; 2. facts; 3. suggestions for improvements. 2. Research facts about plastic pollution of the oceans. Make notes, then rewrite these as paragraphs for a double-page spread. Proofread your work.		

Lesson plan

Unit 26: Placing and spacing punctuation: commas, brackets and dashes

	Lesson 1	Lesson 2	Practice
	Class or groups seated at tables	*Class or groups seated at tables*	*Class or groups seated at tables*
Objective	To place and space punctuation correctly: commas to indicate parenthesis.	To place and space punctuation correctly: commas and dashes.	To place and space punctuation correctly: commas, dashes and brackets.
Resources	– Practice Book Page 28 Part 1 – Presentation Part 1 – Pencil or pen	– Practice Book Page 28 Part 2 – Presentation Part 2 – Pencil or pen	– Additional Practice sheet 26 – Presentation Part 3 – Pencil or pen – Handwriting book or lined paper
Teaching	• **Settling routine and hand warm up** • Use presentation to demonstrate words. • **Paired Talk:** Discuss the meaning of these words and where you might use this punctuation. • **Practice Book:** Copy the words. • Use presentation to discuss the spacing of commas in the sentence. There should be a space after the comma. • Use presentation to read and introduce task: Underline the additional information in each sentence. Rewrite the passage, inserting the commas for parenthesis. • **Practice Book:** Copy the passage, placing and spacing the commas for parenthesis.	• **Settling routine** • Use presentation to demonstrate words. • **Practice Book:** Copy the words. • Remind children that commas and dashes alter the spacing of the words. For example: *The suns – there were three of them, by the way – were beating down.* Draw attention to the spacing. • Use presentation to introduce the task: Space the sentences correctly. • **Practice Book:** Copy the paragraph, spacing the punctuation correctly.	• **Settling routine** • Use presentation to demonstrate words. • **Additional Practice sheet:** Children copy the words. • Remind the children: *Although we are practising commas, dashes and brackets together, they can make writing seem very disjointed and difficult to read if used too often.* • Use presentation to read and introduce task. • Copy the passage, taking extra care with the spacing of the punctuation.
Assessment criterion	Can the children: – place and space punctuation correctly: commas?	– place and space punctuation correctly: commas and dashes?	– place and space punctuation: commas, brackets and dashes?
Further practice	Can the children place and space commas, brackets and dashes correctly in free writing? You can ask the children to do these activities: 1. Write a list of your family, your friends or your pets with a dash followed by some extra information, for example: Mum – the cleverest woman in the world! 2. Write the next paragraph of the science fiction story, including some commas, dashes or brackets. For example: *The creature, who was now shaking with laughter, stepped to one side, and beckoned for them to follow.*		

Happy Handwriting

Lesson plan

Unit 27: Writing quickly: instructions

	Lesson 1	Lesson 2	Practice
Objective	*Class or groups seated at tables* To write quickly and accurately – memorising instructions.	*Class or groups seated at tables* To practise writing quickly and accurately – memorising instructions.	*Class or groups seated at tables* To consolidate writing quickly and accurately – memorising instructions.
Resources	– Practice Book Page 29 Part 1 – Presentation Part 1 – Pencil or pencil – Timer	– Practice Book Page 29 Part 2 – Presentation Part 2 – Pencil or pencil – Timer	– Additional Practice sheet 27 – Presentation Part 3 – Pencil or pencil – Timer – Handwriting book or lined paper
Teaching	• **Settling routine and hand warm up** • Use presentation to demonstrate words. • **Practice Book:** Copy the words. • **Paired Talk:** Use presentation to prompt discussion: *If we write something down, however quickly, it helps us to remember it. When might this be useful? Why must it be legible?* Use presentation to read through the list of instructions. • **Practice Book:** Set the timer. Copy the instructions quickly, making a mark after one minute. Can you remember the instructions? • **Evaluation:** *I can write _____ readable words per minute.*	• **Settling routine** • Use presentation to demonstrate words. • **Paired Talk:** Discuss the meaning of these words. • **Practice Book:** Copy the words. • Use presentation to read through the list of instructions. • **Practice Book:** Set the timer. Copy the instructions quickly, making a mark after one minute. Can you remember the instructions? • **Evaluation:** *I can write _____ readable words per minute.*	• **Settling routine** • Use presentation to demonstrate words. • **Additional Practice sheet:** Children copy the words. • **Paired Talk:** Discuss if the children can still remember the safety instructions for the sea, rivers and canals. • Use presentation to read through the list of instructions and introduce assessment. • Set the timer. Copy the instructions quickly, making a mark after one minute. Can you remember the instructions? • **Evaluation:** *I can write _____ readable words per minute.*
Assessment criterion	Can the children: – write instructions quickly, accurately and legibly when timing themselves?	– write instructions quickly, accurately and legibly when timing themselves?	– write instructions quickly, accurately and legibly when timing themselves?
Further practice	Can the children write quickly, fluently and legibly when writing against the clock? You can ask the children to do these activities: 1. Turn your quick notes into a Summer Safety poster, using your neatest writing and illustrations. 2. Research other information for safety in warmer weather. Make quick notes, then display the information on a poster, for example: pet safety; food hygiene safety; holiday safety.		

Happy Handwriting

Lesson plan

Unit 28: Writing neatly

	Lesson 1	Lesson 2	Practice
	Class or groups seated at tables	*Class or groups seated at tables*	*Class or groups seated at tables*
Objective	To write neatly in a formal document.	To write neatly in a formal document.	To turn quick notes into neat formal writing.
Resources	– Practice Book Page 30 Part 1 – Presentation Part 1 – Pencil	– Practice Book Page 30 Part 2 – Presentation Part 2 – Pencil	– Additional Practice sheet 28 – Presentation Part 3 – Pencil – Handwriting book or lined paper
Teaching	• Settling routine and hand warm up • Use presentation to demonstrate words. • **Practice Book:** Copy the words. • **Paired Talk:** Use presentation to discuss the question: *When might it be important to write very neatly, using our best joined writing?* • Use presentation to read and discuss the handwritten report. • **Practice Book:** Copy the report in their neatest joined handwriting.	• Settling routine • Use presentation to demonstrate words. • **Practice Book:** Copy the words. • **Paired Talk:** Discuss the verb 'to practise' and the noun '(some) practice'. • Use presentation to read the passage and introduce the task: Class 6L has written a report for their teacher. Copy this in their neatest handwriting. • **Practice Book:** Copy the report as neatly as possible.	• Settling routine • Use presentation to demonstrate sentence. • **Additional Practice sheet:** Children copy this sentence. • **Paired Talk:** *Why is it important to have both 'quick writing' and 'neat writing'?* • Use presentation to introduce the task: Here are some very quick notes a teacher has made for a school report. Practise saying these notes as full sentences and then write the report as neatly as you can. • **Practice Book:** Use the notes to write this report in full, as neatly as possible.
Assessment criterion	Can the children: – write neatly when required?	– write neatly when required?	– turn quick notes into neat formal writing?
Further practice	Can the children write neatly when required in formal writing? You can ask the children to do these activities: 1. Make notes on an event, or something you are interested in, then write it out in full to be displayed. 2. Choose a favourite song or poem, write it out in your neatest writing and illustrate it. Perhaps you could frame it for the wall?		

Unit 29: Proofreading, editing and improving

	Lesson 1	Lesson 2	Practice
	Class or groups seated at tables	*Class or groups seated at tables*	*Class or groups seated at tables*
Objective	To revise proofreading.	To practise editing and improving.	To practise proofreading, editing and improving.
Resources	– Practice Book Page 31 Part 1 – Presentation Part 1 – Pencil or pen	– Practice Book Page 31 Part 2 – Presentation Part 2 – Pencil	– Additional Practice sheet 29 – Presentation Part 3 – Pencil – Handwriting book or lined paper
Teaching	• **Settling routine and hand warm up** • Use presentation to demonstrate words. • **Practice Book:** Copy the words. • **Paired Talk:** *What is the difference between proofreading and editing?* Proofreading – looks at misspellings, punctuation, inconsistencies; editing – looks at sentence construction, ideas, effect, vocabulary, clarity, sense. • Use presentation to introduce the task: Proofread the paragraph and rewrite it correctly. • **Practice Book:** Proofread the paragraph and rewrite it correctly.	• **Settling routine** • Use presentation to demonstrate words. • **Practice Book:** Copy the words. • **Paired Talk:** *Why is it necessary to edit your work? How could you improve this passage?* – *I like swimming. I really like swimming at the pool. I like it because it is outside. It's really nice there.* – *I like swimming, and I particularly enjoy visiting the fabulous open-air pool.* • Use presentation to read and introduce the task: Edit and improve the passage. • **Practice Book:** Edit and improve the passage.	• **Settling routine** • Use presentation to demonstrate words. • **Additional Practice sheet:** Children copy the words. • **Paired Talk:** Suggest synonyms and antonyms for *'lovely'*. For example: *wonderful fabulous terrible awful*. • Use presentation to introduce task: Proofread the advert and then edit it. Rewrite it into handwriting books or onto lined paper. • Proofread the passage, then edit it to produce a much improved advert.
Assessment criterion	Can the children: – proofread, looking for misspellings, punctuation and inconsistencies?	– edit, looking for sentence construction, ideas, effect, vocabulary, clarity, sense?	– proofread and edit separately?
Further practice	Can the children proofread and edit when required? You can ask children to do these activities: 1. Write a poem or description of the summer. Proofread and edit it. 2. Write an advert for your village, town, city, country. Why should people come and visit? Proofread it, then go back and edit it to make it sound fantastic.		

Unit 30: Self-assessment

Lesson plan

	Lesson 1	Lesson 2	Practice
Objective	*Class or groups seated at tables* To assess: horizontal joins from *o*, *v* and *w*; spacing of commas and semi-colons within sentences; the height of capital letters.	*Class or groups seated at tables* To assess: legibility, accuracy and fluency of speed writing.	*Class or groups seated at tables* To assess the quality, accuracy and style of my neat writing, recognise improvements and plan next steps.
Resources	– Practice Book Page 32 Part 1 – Presentation Part 1 – Pencil or pen	– Practice Book Page 32 Part 2 – Presentation Part 2 – Pencil or pen – 1 minute timer	– Presentation Part 3 – Pencil – Handwriting book or lined paper
Teaching	• **Settling routine** • Use presentation to discuss the sentence. • Draw attention to tricky joins and joins to round letters; the placing and spacing of comas for parenthesis and the height of capital letters. • Use presentation to read the passage and introduce task. • **Practice Book:** Copy this passage. • Use presentation to introduce assessment. Ask children to assess the formation and spacing of tricky joins; placing and spacing of commas for parenthesis; the height of capital letters.	• **Settling routine** • Use presentation to introduce the task: Set the timer. Copy the autobiography as quickly as you can. Make a mark after one minute, then complete the passage. • **Practice Book:** Copy the passage. • Use presentation to introduce assessment. Ask children to assess the legibility of their speed writing and record the number of words per minute.	• **Settling routine** • Use presentation to introduce activity. Children to copy the poem as neatly as possible, focusing on style and appearance, then complete the self-assessment sentences. • Use presentation to introduce evaluation and next steps: *This term, I have improved at …* *I need to practise …*
Assessment criterion	**Can the children:** – evaluate their handwriting accurately when focusing on: the formation and spacing of tricky joins; placing and spacing of commas for parenthesis; the height of capital letters?	– assess their handwriting accurately when focusing on: legibility and fluency of speed writing?	– assess their handwriting accurately when focusing on: the quality, accuracy and style of their neat writing? – recognise improvements and plan next steps?
Further practice	Do the children need more handwriting practice in free writing? You can ask the children to do these activities: 1. Write a verse from your favourite summer song and illustrate it. 2. Make a card for a teacher and find a suitable thank you poem to write inside. Or better still – write one yourself.		

Name: _____   Unit 1: **Writing quickly and writing neatly**

Set the timer. Copy this limerick twice into your book or onto lined paper.
1. Neatly – don't rush, but time how long it takes.
2. Speedily – time how long it takes.

Compare the two versions.

There was a young teacher called Nessy,
Whose handwriting always looked messy,
Try as she might,
She could not get it right,
So the pupils wrote better than Nessy.

---✂

Name: _____   Unit 2: **My handwriting style and writing f**

Copy these letter combinations three times, slanting your writing.

af   of
fo   fl

Complete the tongue-twister with the words below. Then copy it into your book or onto lined paper.

| followed   flew   farmyard   frightening |

Five fat flies _____ round the farmyard,
_____ the farmer's friends.
The farmer's friends fled out of the _____
_____ by the frightening fat flies.

Happy Handwriting 6: Additional practice sheet   © HarperCollinsPublishers Ltd. 2022

Name: _____   Unit 3: *Joining to and from r*

Copy these letter combinations three times.

or   ro
ar   er

Match the joke and copy them neatly into your book.

Doctor, Doctor, I feel like a pair of curtains.	I see your point.
Doctor, Doctor, I feel like a needle.	I'm afraid I can't see you now.
Doctor, Doctor, I think I'm invisible.	Pull yourself together.

Name: _____   Unit 4: *Slanting key joins: diagonal joins*

Copy these letter combinations three times.

al   um
un   up

Copy this passage into your book or onto lined paper.

The final verdict

The Judge stated that he had never seen such an unpleasant and unlikeable person as... Mr W Cutter! He said that Mr Cutter had taken an instant dislike to poor Mr Wolf and made his life unbearable.

Name: _____   Unit 5: *Keeping ascenders and descenders parallel*

Copy these letter combinations three times.

fl   ng
ly   ky

Copy this poem into your book or onto lined paper.

A sloth sleeps lazily, high in the trees,
Butterflies float on a warm, scented breeze,
Scarlet frogs dance, orangutans play,
Snakes slink silently, stalking their prey.
Fires rage constantly – a blanket of ash,
The sky turns black and majestic trees crash.

Name: _____   Unit 6: *Sentence types*

Copy these words.

statement _____   question _____
command _____   exclamation _____

Punctuate these sentences and identify the sentence type in brackets.
Take care with spacing around capital letters, ? and !

why are basketball players so tall (_____)

it is obvious who is the best player (_____)

don't run when you are holding the ball (_____)

what a great result that was (_____)

do you practise every week (_____)

Name: _____   Unit 7: **Writing quickly: words per minute**

Copy these words.

dangerous _____   shy _____
fearsome _____   friendly _____

Set a one-minute timer. Copy and complete this passage quickly, choosing suitable words. Make a mark when the timer reaches one minute. Complete the passage.

Have you heard of a fangalator? It is an extremely _____ creature that is only found in the deepest oceans. It has four _____ eyes, a _____ tail and scales the colour of _____.

Evaluation: I can write _____ readable words per minute.

Name: _____   Unit 8: **Writing neatly: a formal message**

Copy these words.

ceremony _____   welcome _____
hospitality _____ celebrations _____

Copy and complete the formal letter from the famous author following his visit. Choose appropriate words to complete the passage.

> honoured   celebrations   magnificent
> splendid   sincerely

Dear staff and pupils of Dunkerly School,

Thank you for inviting me to your _____.

I felt _____ to have been asked and, it was _____ to revisit.

Happy Handwriting 6: Additional practice sheet   © HarperCollinsPublishers Ltd. 2022

Name: _____   Unit 9: **Writing brief notes about an event**

Copy these words.

safely _____   returned _____

investigation _____   determine _____

Writing neatly, copy and complete the update on the event for the local news website into your book or onto lined paper.

> ramblings   sedated   investigation   enclosure
> exciting   returned   specialised

Sydney, the six-year-old lion, has been _____ to his _____ at the reserve, none the worse for his _____. He was _____ by the rescue reserve vet and returned in a _____ vehicle. A local resident said, "I'm glad he is back where he should be, but it was quite _____." Meanwhile, an _____ is underway to determine how Sydney escaped."

Name: _____   Unit 11: *Spacing key joins: horizontal joins*

Copy these prefixes three times.

pre   under

over   non

Complete your own restaurant review choosing from the words in the list.

| undercooked   precooked   overcooked |
| nonexistent   horrible   rubbery |

Sorrento is a terrible restaurant! Everything was _____. The pizza was _____; the pasta was _____. The olives were _____, the sauces were _____ and it tasted _____.

Name: _____   Unit 12: *Joining and breaking for descenders*

Copy these words.

carefully _____   quickly _____

adequately _____   mysteriously _____

Copy this weather forecast into your book or onto lined paper.

Here is the weather forecast for the coming week: The country will experience tropical temperatures in the next few days. The Jet Stream, which is drifting up through Europe, could bring highs of over thirty degrees. So, fill up the paddling pool and fire up the barbeque. It's going to be hot!

Name: _____   Unit 13: **Writing words with qu**

Copy these words.

quick _____   quiet _____

square _____   squashed _____

Copy and complete this poem into your book by adding two similes and a title.

A giant key turns in a giant lock.
Gone are the queues, which have clung to the walls all day, like _____.
Gone, the quick-footed tourists, who trampled the gardens, like _____.
And in the quiet night, the ancient castle sleeps.

Name: _____   Unit 14: **Apostrophes in contractions**

Copy these contractions three times.

who'll   who's
what's   where's

Make this diary entry more informal by rewriting it using contractions for the words underlined.

Hi Diary,
I am tired so I will keep this brief. We have been to Gran's! I would have liked to stay, she does not have a spare room. She is moving house and she has promised that I will have my own room. It will be great. She does not break her promises.

Happy Handwriting 6: Additional practice sheet   © HarperCollinsPublishers Ltd. 2022

Name: _____   Unit 15: *Getting the height right: capital letters*

Copy these country initials three times.

UK   USA
UAE   SA

Do you know what the initials stand for?

Copy this travel poem into your book or onto lined paper. Can you find the cities and countries in an atlas?

I've travelled round the world,
And I've sailed across the seas.
Monaco, Mexico, Belgium and Belize.
Germany, Tuscany, Brittany too,
Amsterdam, Rotterdam, Paris and Peru.

Name: _____   Unit 16: *Commas and semi-colons*

Copy this sentence, taking care to place and space the commas.

I bought a jumper, a pair of jeans, and a hoodie.

Rewrite this online review, spacing the punctuation correctly.

The bakery,which has just opened,sells the best bread.I bought some French bread, some soda bread, and some crusty rolls.I couldn't resist the cakes either.There were doughnuts,custard tarts,and blueberry muffins.I bought one of each. Not all for me of course!

Name: _____   Unit 17: *Writing quickly: making notes*

Copy these words.

select _____   key _____
information _____   memory _____

Underline key words and information. Set a timer and write notes as quickly as you can into your book. Use your notes to retell the information to a friend.

Skateboarding started in California in the 1940s or 50s. Surfers wanted something to do when waves were flat. Boards were made of wood with roller-skate wheels attached. It was originally called 'sidewalk surfing' and riders were barefoot.

Name: _____   Unit 18: *Writing neatly and printing*

Copy these words.

printing _____   capital _____
spacing _____   publicity _____

Here is the information for a pantomime. Print the information clearly, spacing it on the page, to create a clear, informative and eye-catching poster to advertise the event.
Note the different sizes of print and use of capital letters.

DICK WHITTINGTON AND HIS CAT

The story of a boy's quest to make his fortune.

OPENING APRIL 1ST (Oh yes it is!)

APOLLO THEATRE Box Office open NOW!

Hurry – tickets are selling fast!

Name: _____   Unit 19: **Alphabetical order: advanced**

Copy these words.

author _____   surname _____

library _____   fiction _____

Write these popular children's authors in alphabetical order, by surname first.

David Wiesner   Marcia Williams   David Walliams
Jaqueline Wilson   Tom Watson   Anna Wilson
Alex Williams   Steve Williams   Joe Wilson

Happy Handwriting 6: Additional practice sheet   © HarperCollinsPublishers Ltd. 2022

Name: _____ Unit 21: *Spacing key joins: compound words*

Copy these words.

rust-covered _____

well-known _____

Play 'Hyphen or No Hyphen?'.
Decide whether the compound words should have a 'hyphen or no hyphen', then rewrite this story opening into your book.

Zac stepped out into the pitchblack. The farmyard was dark after the brightlylit kitchen. Suddenly a fastmoving figure appeared against the barn. It turned to face him, greeneyed and fiercelooking, then wagged its whitetipped tail.

Name: _____ Unit 22: *Slanting your writing*

Copy these words.

appeal _____   urgent _____

volunteer _____   grateful _____

Copy this photocopied note into your book, taking care to slant your writing to the right.

Urgent appeal!
Staff are seeking fancy dress items for the Summer Fair. The theme is Superheroes, so any coloured tights, capes or masks would be gratefully received. Staff also want crash courses in flying. (Non-crash courses would be even better!)

Name: _____   Unit 23: **Revising key joins: joins to round letters**

Copy these words.

apologise _____   apply _____

address _____   dangerous _____

Copy this poem into your book, taking extra care to join round letters accurately and break after p and g.

The Tennis Match

The pendulum swings, first left and then right,

The green of the court, the players in white.

The gasping for breath, the cheer of the fans,

The scoring of points, and raising of hands.

Name: _____   Unit 24: **Spacing tricky joins**

Copy these words.

super _____   third _____

after _____   faster _____

Copy and complete this reference into your book.

> respectful offer perfect rarely terrific forgets

Zafira would be a _____ form monitor. She is friendly, _____ and hard-working. She is _____ late and never _____ her homework. She would _____ support to others and be a _____ role model.

Happy Handwriting 6: Additional practice sheet   © HarperCollinsPublishers Ltd. 2022

Name: _____   Unit 25: **Proofreading and paragraphing**

Copy these words.

subject _____   sentence _____

connection _____   topic _____

Proofread and rewrite this biography in two paragraphs: Introduction, and Outcome.

In january 2017, on arlian ecker's birthday, he saw rehabilitated sea turtles released into the ocean they had been hurt by plastic pollution. He began researching, writing blogs and educating young people like himself. Now, he has created a new superhero – Plastic Free Boy!

Name: _____   Unit 26: **Commas, brackets and dashes**

Copy these words.

spacing _____   placing _____

separating _____   adding _____

Copy this passage into your book, taking extra care with the spacing of the punctuation.

Lucas and Min (not the bravest of people) moved closer to Sofia. The creature, whose grin was like a watermelon slice, began to make a strange sound. The three friends, feeling very confused, glanced at each other. Suddenly, they all realised – the creature was laughing!

Name: _____ Unit 27: **Writing quickly: instructions**

Copy these words.

instructions _____ speed _____

safety _____ memorise _____

Set a one minute timer. Write the instructions quickly, making a mark after one minute.

Stay safe this summer – sun

1. Always use sunscreen of SPF 30 or higher.
2. Avoid the day's strongest rays, around noon.
3. Cover up where possible, or sit in the shade.
4. Wear a hat when the sun is strong.
5. Wear sunglasses and NEVER look at the sun.

Name: _____ Unit 28: **Writing neatly**

Copy this sentence.

Neat writing takes longer.

Below are some quick notes a teacher has written for a school report. Practise saying these notes as full sentences, and then write the report as neatly as you can into your book.

Ron pleasant friendly hard working; improvement

English – great vocab; handwriting – style clear
    – spelling – good; grammar – needs work

Mathematics – strength; enjoys; grasps new concepts
    – quickly/ easily

Science – knowledgeable; likes practical experiments

Name: _____   Unit 29: **Proofreading, editing and improving**

Copy these words.

synonyms _____   antonyms _____

vocabulary _____   develop _____

Proofread this advert for a holiday destination and then edit it. Rewrite it and improve it.

Visit veladu this summer! It is really nice. it has got a nice beech with a lot of sand. it is really long and clean and really big. the see is clean and really safe and you can swim or get a boat or a pedaloes or a sunshades. there are lots of lovely stall with lots of colours on them stalls selling lots of nice food and there are lots of lovely shops selling things you might need fot the beech.

Assessing handwriting in Year 6

There are a number of types of assessment of handwriting:

- statutory summative assessment – to compare pupil performance with national expectations and comparisons
- day-to-day formative assessment – to inform teaching on an ongoing basis
- diagnostic assessment – to identify particular strengths and weaknesses
- in-school summative assessment – to understand pupil performance at the end of a period of teaching.

Assessing handwriting in the National Curriculum – the end of Key Stage 2

Teacher Assessment

At the end of Key Stage 2, teachers must assess using the Teacher Assessment Frameworks. These holistic assessments include the following handwriting requirements:

- Working towards the expected standard: The pupil can write legibly, although not necessarily in a joined hand.
- Working at the expected standard: The pupil maintains legibility in joined handwriting when writing at speed.

The National Curriculum states that pupils should be taught to 'write legibly, fluently and with increasing speed by choosing which shape of a letter to use when given choices and deciding whether or not to join specific letters; choosing the writing implement that is best suited for a task'.

These goals are also the basis of in-school summative assessment, which may use the day-to-day assessments of handwriting you make in your class and the children's self-assessment at the end of each term, to inform your judgement.

Day-to-day assessment of handwriting in your class in Year 6

To make an overall assessment of children's handwriting at Year 6, it is important to consider both the product of their writing and the way they do the writing. We suggest that comprehensive assessment of handwriting in Year 6 includes:

- scrutiny of a sample of children's written notes, or informal writing, written at some speed
- scrutiny of a sample of children's final draft or presentation writing.

The handwriting example record sheet on page 67 will support your assessment.

When assessing each piece of writing consider:

- Is the writing legible, to a degree that suits its purpose? (5 = easily read, 1 = unable to read)
- Are the letters regular in size and spacing? (5 = very regular, 1 = very erratic)
- Is there evidence of flow in the joining? (5 = well joined flow, 1 = no joins)
- Are letter height and joins consistent? (5 = very consistent, 1 = very erratic)
- Are letters and words appropriate in size and position? (5 = all relatively appropriate, 1 = very varied)
- Are short letters, ascenders and descenders in the correct proportions? (5 = all correct proportions, 1 = ascenders indistinguishable)

Fluent, legible and speedy handwriting in Year 6 is based on correct letter formation and correct joining between letters. To know whether children have formed a letter or join correctly you need see them do it. Observation of the act of writing is vital, especially where children are struggling. Observe handwriting when using the Practice Book and also in children's free writing. In Year 6, you should also observe the degree to which children's handwriting is legible when written speedily. When children are writing more quickly, you should also note which letters or joins cause hesitation, as these need further practice.

A general assessment record sheet for Year 6 handwriting is on page 68 of this guide. In Year 6, you may also want to record which letter formations children can use and which ones require more practice.

The use of joins should be becoming automatic in Year 6 but for a few children this will remain a challenging goal. Facilitating this will enable the children to compose what they want to say more freely, so it is worth the effort to arrange additional practice. An assessment record sheet for joins between letters in Year 6 is on page 69 of this guide.

In addition, the *Happy Handwriting* printable resources include more detailed assessment and practice materials which you will find useful for students who need particular handwriting support:

- Year 6 extra support activity sheets for the formation of letter families
- Year 6 extra assessment sheets for diagonal joins, horizontal joins and joins to round letters.

Self-assessment of handwriting

Understanding the criteria for 'good' handwriting is very important, and these criteria change as children go through their education. In Year 6, all children should be able to form all letters correctly and be secure in forming joins. Size, orientation and spacing of letters should be largely under control and children are learning to choose whether to write quickly, or with full attention to neatness. In either case, writers should aim for legible text.

Talking about these criteria during handwriting lessons is important and the full glossary in the printable resources will be useful. Whenever children complete handwriting practice, it is a good idea to ask them to consider how well they achieved their handwriting goals and identify what they still find difficult in handwriting. The lessons in Weeks 10, 20 and 30 are designed to support children to self-evaluate their handwriting. You could also ask them to consider their writing in another context to evaluate how much of their success at handwriting lessons is evident.

Diagnostic assessment of handwriting

A small proportion of children in Year 6 will benefit from a more in-depth assessment of their handwriting to enable them to make progress, and when you have identified what aspects of handwriting are particularly challenging individuals or groups you will be able to use the *Happy Handwriting* materials to provide additional practice for these children.

At Year 6, automatic, correct formation of letters remains vital, and is an underlying priority for all children if they are to write legibly, but a few may still struggle with this. Joining letters automatically is the next most important priority. Other aspects of effective handwriting, identified in the assessment guidance above, include spacing and speed. These aspects of handwriting depend on good, automatic formation and joining. You can assess the handwriting of children who appear to be struggling and offer individuals or groups of children additional practice which will help them to improve a particular aspect of their handwriting. This will help them become automatic in their writing and reduce the amount of attention they have to give this basic aspect of their learning.

Use the diagnostic assessment of handwriting sheet on page 70 and the instructions below to do a diagnostic assessment. The assessment should be done in small groups with an adult to give clear instructions and observe the letter formation used by children as they complete the sheet. The diagnostic assessment sheet includes three short tasks: copying a sentence, a free writing task and writing out the alphabet from memory. Observe these tasks and decide whether each child can:

- form letters correctly and consistently, without hesitation, when they copy the sentences.
- form letters correctly and consistently, without hesitation when they write a sentence, they are composing themselves.
- join the letters correctly and consistently in the copying task and composing task (and which joins they use).
- write out the lower-case alphabet from memory at least once, without hesitation within a minute.

Until children in Year 6 are able to produce letters automatically, they will struggle to join letters or write quickly. For some children, joining letters will always be difficult and at Year 6 you may need to choose a particular focus for handwriting practice. If a struggling writer is having difficulty with automatic letter production and joining letters, it is most important that they can produce the letters automatically and consistently. This should remain the most basic handwriting priority because it will help them most with their composition.

Doing the additional practice activities on the sheets in this Teacher's Guide, the further practice suggestions in each week's planning grid, the targeted sheets in the Teacher's Guide, and the printable resources allows you to offer plenty of opportunities for practice of the aspects of handwriting children need.

Instructions for diagnostic assessment

The copying task

Ask the children to copy the sentences as quickly and legibly as they can, onto the sheet within 10 minutes. The copying task for Year 6 includes the classic sentence which contains all the letters of the alphabet, so you can see which ones the children can join.

Observe the children as they copy the sentences on the sheet. Identify the letters the child writes incorrectly, inconsistently or hesitates before writing. These letters need to be learned more thoroughly as a movement. Observe which joins are used, cause the child to pause, or are incorrect. The revision sheets in the printable resources can be used to support improvement in letter formation. We recommend practice focused on the letters causing difficulty, rather than repeating all the letters. The speed and fluency practice sheets on pages 71, 72 and 73 should be used to promote automatic letter production.

The free writing task

Ask the children to compose a piece of writing about their favourite meal. Give the children 10 minutes to do this task in an exercise book or on paper, and consider how much they write as part of the assessment.

It is important to observe free writing because you aim to be sure that, when composing text, children still maintain efficient handwriting when other parts of the writing process demand attention. Again, the aim is to identify any letters or joins children do not form correctly, that they form inconsistently, or which cause them to hesitate (a sure sign the movement is not automatic).

The free writing and copying tasks should be completed within 10 minutes. If children can only produce a very few words, this suggests that they need more letter production practice to improve their handwriting speed – the speed and fluency practice sheets can be useful for very slow writers.

The alphabet writing task – automatic letter production

Ask children to: *Please write out the letters of the alphabet, in lower case, as quickly and neatly as possible. If you complete writing the alphabet, start again until I say 'stop'*. Give the children one minute to write the alphabet. After a minute say 'stop'.

This is an activity to test how quickly the children can produce a well-known sequence of letters (the alphabet), so it is only useful if the children know the alphabet reasonably well. We would expect all children to be able to write out the alphabet in less than a minute by the start of Year 3, and in Year 6 we would expect them to be able to do so neatly and legibly. If children struggle to produce letters automatically, use the speed and fluency practice sheets to improve automatic letter production. These activities work by asking the children to repeatedly write unpredictable combinations of letters. The unusual combinations of letters mean the writers have to repeatedly bring the letter formation to mind, which helps to fix them in memory.

Activities to promote automatic letter production

The speed and fluency practice sheets (pages 71, 72 and 73) aim to promote automatic writing of letters without children having to actively think about the letter movement. Where children cannot do this, traditional practice of writing out rows of the same letters, or predictable letter combinations, do not help very much. To improve automatic writing of letters, children should practise unlikely and unexpected combinations of letters which force them to 'bring to mind' the letter shape and movement quickly. You can use some simple school equipment to do a small number of activities which give children practice. These are best done with groups of children in short, intense lessons. You will need:

- a timing device for one, two and three minutes
- spinners, magnetic letters, etc.
- alphabet letter cards (from the printable resources)
- paper and pencil.

Letter spinner: One child is the 'timer' and one child is the 'spinner' in each round. The 'spinner' spins two or three letter spinners and calls out the letter names. The 'timer' times one minute and the children in the group have to write out the letters 'called' as a sequence as many times as they can in one minute, saying the letter name as they write it. This helps to fix the letter movement and name in memory.

Feelie bag letters: One student is the 'timer' and one student is the 'caller' in each round. The 'caller' pulls two or three letters out of the bag (or box) and calls out the letter names. The 'timer' times one minute and the children in the group have to write out the letters 'called' as many times as they can in one minute, saying the letter name as they write it. This helps to fix the letter movement and name in memory.

Letter cards: One student is the 'dealer' and one student is the 'timer' in each round. The 'dealer' deals three letter cards and says their name. The children in the group have to write that combination of letters as many times as they can in the minute timed by the 'timer'. This helps to fix the visual representation of the letter.

Handwriting example record sheet

Child's name	Legibility (5 = easily read, 1 = unable to read)	Regular in size and spacing (5 = very regular, 1 = very erratic)	Flow in the joining (5 = well joined flow, 1 = no joins)	Letter height and joins are consistent (5 = very consistent, 1 = very erratic)	Letters and words are appropriate in size and position (5 = all relatively appropriate, 1 = very varied)	Writes short letters, ascenders and descenders in the correct proportions (5 = all correct proportions, 1 = ascenders indistinguishable)	Total
1							
2							
3							
4							
5							
6							
7							
8							
9							
10							
11							
12							
13							
14							
15							
16							
17							
18							
19							
20							
21							
22							
23							
24							
25							
26							
27							
28							
29							
30							

Happy Handwriting

Assessment record sheet for Year 6 handwriting

Child name	Sits appropriately with feet and shoulders straight	Starts letters at the right place	Makes the correct letter movement without hesitation	Consistently uses the correct letter movement wherever the letter occurs	Keeps the pencil on the paper between joined letters	Writes short letters, ascenders and descenders in the correct proportions	Makes target joins between letters in the Practice Book	Uses target joins in their own writing	Knows the names and order of letters in the alphabet
1									
2									
3									
4									
5									
6									
7									
8									
9									
10									
11									
12									
13									
14									
15									
16									
17									
18									
19									
20									
21									
22									
23									
24									
25									
26									
27									
28									
29									
30									

Assessment record sheet for joins in Year 6

Name/group name: Date:

Can the child...	Diagonal joins to letters without ascenders	Diagonal joins to letters with ascenders	Horizontal joins to letters without ascenders	Horizontal joins to letters with ascenders	Joins to round (anti-clockwise) letters
	Diagonal join to short letter	Diagonal join to tall letter	Horizontal join to short letter	Horizontal join to tall letter	Joins to round letters
	im re an ra	*ake th all ef*	*or wa fa ve*	*wh ot ot*	*ed ing ra*
Consistently make the correct letter movement for each unjoined letter?					
Form letters without hesitation?					
Keep the pencil on the paper for the whole letter movement?					
Make the correct join movement?					
Maintain appropriate proportions of ascender and short letter?					
Keep the pencil on the paper for the whole sequence of joined letters?					
Write joined sequences without hesitation?					

Name/Group: _____   Date: _____

Diagnostic assessment of handwriting

Copy the sentences quickly and neatly.

The quick brown fox jumped over the lazy dog.

He had to get out of the garden before the dog

finally stirred himself and saw.

But the food in that dustbin was delicious!

Write three or four sentences about 'my favourite meal' below.
Tell the reader what you would like to eat, and who you would like to share it with.

Write out the alphabet in lower-case letters as quickly as you can, but make sure the letters are readable.

Name/Group: _____   Date: _____

Speed and fluency practice sheet: Curly Caterpillar Letters

This sheet will help you to practise letters so you can write them automatically.

Write over then copy the letter pattern as quickly as you can.
Say the letter name as you write it.

ae ae

co co

dg dg

se fe

ged ged

esf esf

dca dca

cfoq

qacf

faos

aoeg

Name/Group: _____ Date: _____

Speed and fluency practice sheet: Long Ladder Letters

This sheet will help you to practise letters so you can write them automatically.

Write over then copy the letter pattern as quickly as you can.
Say the letter name as you write it.

il il

kt kt

uy uy

lt lt

juy juy

ilt ilt

klj klj

ittk ittk

jytl jytl

lult lult

Name/Group: _____   Date: _____

Speed and fluency practice sheet: Robot and Zigzag Letters

This sheet will help you to practise letters so you can write them automatically.

✏️ *Write over then copy the letter pattern as quickly as you can.
Say the letter name as you write it.*

m m
mh mh
hb hb
bp bp

whr whr
wbn wbn
vbn vbn
rwm rwm

xhnr xhnr
nmbp nmbp
whnr whnr

Name/Group: _____   Date: _____

Extra practice sheet: diagonal joins

✏️ Warm up by writing a row of this pattern.

alealeale

✏️ Write a row of each of these prefixes.

ante

ex

hyper

inter

post

✏️ Write the prefixes into the spaces and then copy out the words.

_____ script _____ stellar _____ sensitive

____ cavate _____ date

✏️ Copy the sentences.

She longed to join the team excavating this site.

The undergrowth around the ruin was impenetrable.

She would have to intervene to prevent damage.

Name/Group: _____ Date: _____

Extra practice sheet: horizontal joins

Warm up by writing a row of this pattern.

rowrow

Write a row of each of these joins.

on

re

ve

wh

rf

Write over and copy out the words.

why what why wherever whenever whose

Copy the sentences.

"Are you really sure?" Stella asked.

Whenever I see her, I know something is going on.

On this side, we have very little to worry about.

Happy Handwriting 6: Extra practice sheet: horizontal joins © HarperCollinsPublishers Ltd. 2022

Extra practice sheet: joins to round letters

Warm up by writing a row of this pattern.

cadcad

Write a row of each of these joins.

ad

ic

ca

id

ight

Write over and copy out the words.

bright   thought   slid   heard   candle   address

Copy the sentences.

Knowing the address is vital when sending parcels.

There was a fight in the penguin pool of the zoo.

No birds were hurt, but a keeper fell over.

Name/Group: _____   Date: _____

Extra practice sheet: capital letters for proper nouns

Fill in the missing capital letters.

A B C _ _ F G H _ K L _ N O P _ _ S T _ _ W _ Y Z

Write out the letter sequences in capital letters.

lmno _ _ _ _   pqrst _ _ _ _ _

bcde _ _ _ _   mnop _ _ _ _

Correct the names by adding capitals and copy them out.

Miss kaur   sir Monty   dr smith   ms grey   mr benn

Correct this letter by adding capitals and copying it out on a piece of paper.

> the escape room
> cubbington
> br22 fxb
>
> dear mr perrin,
>
> thank you for enquiring about a Saturday job at the escape room. If you are interested in this role, please fill in the attached form and return it by 1st November. We will interview candidates in the week of 20th November.
>
> Sincerely,
>
> Darren marks
>
> Senior manager, The escape room

Guidance for alphabetical order tasks

Alphabet knowledge is one of the strongest predictors of reading success in young learners. Knowing the names of the letters allows us to talk about them and helps with phonics and spelling. It is very useful to be able to be clear whether you mean the letter name c (pronounced *see*) or the sound /c/. If a child says, 'How do I spell /ch/ in *chip*?' The answer 'Using letters c and h' is correct, but the answer 'With the sounds /c/ and /h/' is not. (These sounds do not blend to form /ch/.)

Learning letter names helps children link the lower-case and capital letter. Of course, it is also important to discuss the sounds associated with letters in phonics, and children have no difficulty learning both names and sounds.

Alphabetical order of letter names is an easily memorised sequence that lasts a lifetime. Later in their education, this sequence helps children to use dictionaries and alphabetical order.

We hope all children will know the alphabet and letter names by Year 6, but if you have children in the class who do not, we suggest you do the following to help them learn letter names and alphabetical order:

- Regularly sing the names of all the letters of the alphabet to a known tune. The most common tune is *Twinkle Twinkle Little Star*. Remember to name the last letter 'zed'. This is very important for children who join the class at this age.
- Use the alphabet cards from the printable resources (which can be printed out, laminated and cut up) to play games. Give each child a letter (you may need some duplicates if there are more than 26 in the class). Sing the alphabet song and the holder of each letter jumps up, or sits down, when their letter is sung. This can be adapted to children naming an animal starting with their letter, etc.
- As a class or group, do an alphabet hunt using an alphabet list. Children take it in turns to find a word that begins with the letter and the group leader writes up the list.
- Use the alphabetical order practice sheets to match up lower-case letters and capital letters.
- Use the alphabetical order practice sheets to make lists of items around the school, such as animals. The list of capitals can be used to collect as many names (or place names) as possible.
- Use the alphabet cards to line up for any sort of activity. Children will soon start to recognise the 'section' of the alphabet their letter falls into. When the line is assembled, each child says the letter name on their card in turn.

Writing guidelines

Writing guidelines